Christian Controversy
in Alexandria

American University Studies

Series VII
Theology and Religion
Vol. 172

PETER LANG
New York • Washington, D.C./Baltimore • San Francisco
Bern • Frankfurt am Main • Berlin • Vienna • Paris

Everett Procter

Christian Controversy in Alexandria

Clement's Polemic against the Basilideans and Valentinians

PETER LANG
New York • Washington, D.C./Baltimore • San Francisco
Bern • Frankfurt am Main • Berlin • Vienna • Paris

BR
65
.C66
P75
1995

Library of Congress Cataloging-in-Publication Data

Procter, Everett.
    Christian controversy in Alexandria: Clement's polemic against the
Basilideans and Valentinians / Everett Procter.
       p.   cm. — (American university studies. Series VII, Theology and
religion; vol. 172)
    Includes bibliographical references.
    1. Clement, of Alexandria, Saint. ca. 150-ca. 215. 2. Basilides, fl.
117-140. 3. Valentinus, 2nd cent. 4. Basilideans—Controversial
literature—History and criticism. 5. Valentinians—Controversial
literature—History and criticism. 6. Alexandria (Egypt)—History and
criticism—Early church, ca. 30-600. 7. Egypt—History and criticism—
Early church, ca. 30-600. 8. Apologetics—Early church, ca. 30-600.
I. Title. II. Series.
    BR65.C66P75   273'.1—dc20   93-37342
    ISBN 0-8204-2378-5   CIP
    ISSN 0740-0446

Die Deutsche Bibliothek-CIP-Einheitsaufnahme

Procter, Everett:
Christian controversy in Alexandria: Clement's polemic against the
Basilideans and Valentinians / Everett Procter. - New York; San Francisco;
Bern; Baltimore; Frankfurt am Main; Berlin; Wien; Paris: Lang
    (American university studies: Ser. 7, Theology and religion; Vol. 172)
    ISBN 0-8204-2378-5
NE: American university studies / 07

The paper in this book meets the guidelines for permanence and durability of
the Committee on Production Guidelines for Book Longevity of the
Council on Library Resources.

© Peter Lang Publishing, Inc., New York 1995

To Sharon Berryessa, for her inspiration and support
during the writing of this book.

Acknowledgements

I wish to thank Paul and Marguerite Specht, Katherine Redick, and Lorraine Berryessa for their encouragement and assistance along the way. I also would like to thank the members of my doctoral committee, especially Professor Birger Pearson in Early Christianity and Professor Robert Renehan in Classics, both at the University of California, Santa Barbara.

Table of Contents

Preface

This book is intended for general readers and specialists in the history of early Christianity, Gnosticism, patristics, theology, and classics. Quite often, studies of the ancient church are vexed by the lack of primary sources. The problem is even more acute in the case of people like Basilides, Valentinus, and their disciples, for much of our evidence about their beliefs and practices appears in the writings of their opponents. Fortunately, we have in the extant works of Clement of Alexandria a relatively large number of quotations, summaries, and paraphrases of writing from the Basilideans and Valentinians. In addition, Clement is considered by most scholars to be a trustworthy witness to the teachings of such people, and his comments on their doctrines provide an insider's view of the Christian communities in Alexandria near the end of the second century.

Several scholars have produced excellent studies on Clement of Alexandria, a few of whom are R. Casey, F. Sagnard, H. Chadwick, A. Méhat, and S. Lilla. Some of these investigators also have pointed out certain structural parallels between the ideas of Clement and those of the Basilideans or Valentinians. To my knowledge, no one has made a complete study of Clement's citations from the Basilideans and Valentinians or his response to their doctrines. Therefore, the present book is devoted to that task. I have included my own translations of most of the texts under consideration so that the reader can see the evidence upon which my conclusions are based. Throughout the book I have used a topical arrangement, proceeding from teachings of the various authors on theology, cosmology, and anthropology to their opinions on soteriology, ecclesiology, liturgy, ethics, and eschatology. I owe a debt, of course, to my teachers and other scholars in this field, though whatever errors my work may contain are mine.

Introduction

WITH its excellent harbors, broad thoroughfares, and magnificent public buildings, the city of Alexandria was second in size and importance only to Rome in the first two centuries of the common era. Founded by Alexander the Great and enriched by a succession of Ptolemaic rulers, Alexandria was a place of great industry, commerce, wealth, and cultural diversity. As a port city, it was the major point of transfer for goods moving from the interior of Egypt, Arabia, and the Indies to points in the western part of the Mediterranean basin. The city also was the home of the Museum where artists, poets, and scholars under royal or imperial patronage made great contributions to human civilization in the areas of art, science, literature, and philosophy. Attached to the Museum was one of the largest and best-known libraries in antiquity. The intellectual activity of the Museum and resources of the library brought many educated people to Alexandria and turned the city into a center of learning in which one could receive instruction in the contemporary philosophies of Plato, Aristotle, Epicurus, and the Stoa.[1]

In the Roman imperial period the population of Alexandria was composed of native Egyptians, Greeks, Romans, a large community of Jews, and representatives from other ethnic groups of the surrounding lands. The ethnic diversity of the city's population was reflected in the variety of its religious cults, some of which were located in large, ornately furnished temples. Among the smaller places of worship were the synagogues of the Jews. Situated in two of the five divisions of the ancient city, the Jewish community of Alexandria had produced a Greek translation of the Hebrew scriptures known as the Septuagint and was the home of the religious philosopher and writer, Philo. The Septuagint was destined to become the scripture of the early Christian churches while the works of Philo provided a ready source of ideas for the development of Christian theology in Alexandria at the hands of men like Valentinus, Clement, and Origen. In fact, the first Christian converts in Egypt were probably Alexandrian Jews.[2]

The first Christian in Egypt about whom we have any certain knowledge is Basilides, who lived during the first part of the second century. It has been suggested that before taking up residence in Alexandria, Basilides studied in Antioch of Syria under a Christian teacher by the name of Menander. Whether an immigrant or a native, Basilides was active in Alexandria between the reign of the emperor Hadrian (117-35) and that of Antoninus Pius (135-161). Basilides appears to have established a Christian school, influenced perhaps by the organization and methods of pagan philosophical schools. Besides being a teacher, Basilides also composed commentaries on the scripture and a gospel.[3]

Unfortunately, the whole of Basilides' thought cannot be recovered because only fragments or summaries of his writings have been preserved, and these are recorded in the works of his ecclesiastical opponents, heresiologists like Irenaeus, Clement of Alexandria, and Hippolytus. The genuine fragments of Basilides' writings cited by Clement, however, reveal the work of an eclectic philosopher and theologian seeking to interpret the scripture with the aid of Platonic and Stoic categories.[4]

The school and teachings of Basilides seem to have been maintained by his son and disciple, Isidore. At least one other disciple may have been in Rome around the beginning of the third century, for a monistic interpretation of Basilides' original teachings is recorded in the writings of Hippolytus, a member of the Roman church. As we shall see, some Basilideans of the second generation disagreed with the founder of their school and his son Isidore regarding certain ethical matters. Eventually, the followers of Basilides disappeared from history, partly because of the relative austerity of their teachings and partly because of the polemics brought against them by other Christians.[5]

One of the greatest Christian teachers to come from Egypt was Valentinus. Born in the delta region at the beginning of the second century, he probably was educated and became a convert in Alexandria (c. 117-38). Judging from the extant fragments of his works recorded by Clement, Valentinus was instructed in Platonic philosophy, allegorical interpretation, and a learned and poetic style of writing. He also might have been taught by a man named Theodas, a reputed student of Paul, and have become acquainted with the teachings of Basilides. Undoubtedly, Valentinus met certain Gnostics in Alexandria, for his writings exhibit the radical dualism, denigration of the Jewish creator, and emphasis upon esoteric knowledge that were part of the religiosity of such people. After working perhaps as a Christian teacher in Alexandria, Valentinus travelled to Rome and rose to a position of prominence as a member of one of the churches in that city (c. 140). In Rome, Valentinus might have met Marcion and Justin, two other men who were to play decisive roles in the history of the Christian church.[6]

It is not known for sure whether Valentinus was ever considered for the office of bishop in the city of Rome. We do know, however, that he began to expound his own understanding of Christian belief and practice through a bold and far-reaching allegorical exegesis of the scripture and that he expressed his ideas in philosophical treatises, letters, homilies, and poems. In time other Christians, like Justin, wrote polemical tractates in which they accused Valentinus of being a heretic or teacher of false doctrine. Undaunted by the attacks of his opponents, Valentinus continued to promote his unique brand of Christianity until his death in Rome or on the island of Cyprus (c. 165). Apparently, Valentinus remained a member of the established Christian churches, reserving his radical interpretation of the scripture for selected disciples in a school setting outside the regular worship services.[7]

A number of brilliant teachers and writers carried on the work of Valentinus by bringing their master's doctrines to Christian communities in Gaul, Asia Minor, Syria, Mesopotamia, and Egypt. Since the allegorical method enabled several exegetes to arrive at different conclusions about the meaning of a single text, the disciples of Valentinus added their own insights and speculations to the original doctrine of their teacher, altering it in significant and interesting ways. After a time, two distinct branches or schools of thought emerged from within the Valentinian movement as a whole: the Italic or western school, whose chief representatives were Ptolemy and Heracleon, and the Anatolian or eastern school, which numbered Theodotus and Marcus among its most important leaders. One of the principal differences of opinion between these two Valentinian schools concerned the nature of the body of Jesus. The members of the Italic school held that the body of Jesus was made from a psychic substance while the adherents of the Anatolian school claimed that it was created from a spiritual element akin to the nature of the supreme deity.[8]

Though at first the followers of Valentinus participated in the worship of established Christian churches, they gradually withdrew from these congregations and formed their own communities, spurred on by the increasing criticism of their fellow believers. The polemics against the Valentinians reached a new level of intensity when Irenaeus, the bishop of Lyons, wrote his monumental treatise, the *Adversus Haereses* (c. 180-5). In the latter work Irenaeus endeavored to create a comprehensive definition of correct Christian belief and practice in opposition to the teachings of Basilides, Valentinus, and many others. At about the same time as the publication of Irenaeus's work, a young Christian scholar by the name of Clement arrived in the city of Alexandria and embarked upon studies in a school led by a former Stoic philosopher identified as Pantaenus. In this school Pantaenus taught the essentials of the Christian faith to catechumens in order to prepare them for baptism and gave advanced instruction on scripture, ethics, and theology to those who were already members of the church.[9]

Clement himself had been born to pagan parents in Athens or Alexandria (c. 150) and had gone in search of instruction from several teachers in Greece, Magna Graecia, and the East after his conversion to Christianity. According to Clement's own testimony, his quest for knowledge ended in Egypt when he discovered the last and greatest of his teachers, Pantaenus. Clement appears to have studied in the school of Pantaenus for about ten years and then to have become head of the same institution following the retirement or death of his master (c. 190). Just before Clement's promotion, a man named Demetrius had been elected bishop of some of the Christian churches in Alexandria. Like Irenaeus and other bishops in the principal cities of the Roman empire,

Demetrius tried to enforce what he considered to be correct Christian teaching in the churches under his authority and to exclude from such congregations those who were deemed purveyors of false or "heretical" doctrine. As part of his program, Demetrius allied himself with and eventually gained control of the catechetical school founded by Pantaenus.[10]

There is little reason to doubt that in his role as head of the catechetical school Clement supported the ecclesiastical work of bishop Demetrius. Indeed, while teaching in the school, Clement began to write a large number of books in which he set forth the beliefs and practices of his own Christian community over against those of certain people whom he regarded as heretics, people like Basilides, Valentinus, and their respective followers. Let us turn now to the material that Clement cites from the Basilideans and Valentinians before moving on to discuss his polemic against it.[11]

Notes

[1] See the excellent description of Alexandria in Tollinton, *Clement of Alexandria*, vol. 1, pp. 31-63.

[2] The lack of primary evidence makes it difficult to know exactly when Christianity came to Egypt. Eusebius' statement about Mark being the first Christian preacher in Egypt and the founder of the church in Alexandria cannot be verified; Eus. *H.E.* 2.16.1. Similarly, there is little historical value in Eusebius' claim that the first Christian converts in Egypt were the ascetic Therapeutae depicted in the works of Philo; Eus. *H.E.* 2.16.2. It is also unlikely that the earliest Christians in Egypt were the Basilideans and Valentinians. In fact, Christian writings like the Gospel of the Hebrews, Gospel of the Egyptians, *Epistle of Barnabas*, and *Preaching of Peter* are known to have been in use in Egypt around the same time that Basilides and Valentinus were active there. Since the aforementioned texts contain no distinctly Basilidean or Valentinian features, they were probably the property of Christians who were not disciples of Basilides and Valentinus. At the present state of research, the most that can be said is that there seems to have been more than one kind of Christian community in Egypt, and particularly Alexandria, by the beginning of the second century.

[3] Basilides is thought to have lived in Alexandria c. 117–61; cf. *Strom.* 7.106.4 (3.75.13–6). On the possibility of Basilides coming from Syria to Alexandria see Pearson, *Gnosticism, Judaism, and Egyptian Christianity*, pp. 202f.; on Basilides composing a gospel see Orig. *Hom. in Luc.* 1 cited in Foerster, *Gnosis*, p. 74, n.17.

[4] Generally, Clement is considered to be a reliable source for the teachings of Basilides. Irenaeus's summary of the teachings of Basilides also appears to be fairly accurate since it coheres somewhat with the reports given by Clement. The Basilidean material described by Hippolytus, however, seems to be the work of a disciple of Basilides because it bears only a superficial resemblance to the material presented by Clement and Irenaeus.

[5] On the reinterpretation of Basilides' original doctrine see Hipp. *Refut.* 7.20.1-27.13 and the discussion in Rudolph, *Gnosis*, pp. 309-12.

[6] On the probable dates of Valentinus's activities see *Strom.* 7.106.4–107.1 (3.75.13–8); Iren. *Adv. Haer.* 3.3.4; 4.3; on Valentinus being taught by Theodas see *Strom.* 7.106.4-107.1 (3.75.15-8); on the possible connection between Valentinus and Basilides see the discussion in Layton, *The Gnostic Scriptures*, p. 417; on the relationship of Valentinus's system of thought to that of the Gnostics see Iren. *Adv. Haer.* 1.11.1; cf. 1.29.1-4; 1.30.1-31.1.

[7] On the writings of Valentinus see the discussion of his treatises, homilies, and letters in chapters 1 and 2 below; on the poetry of Valentinus see Hipp. *Refut.* 6.37.6-8; on Valentinus's bid for the office of bishop see Tert. *Adv. Valent.* 4.1.

[8] On the difference between the Italic and Anatolian views of Jesus' nature see Hipp. *Refut.* 6.35.5-7.

[9] We do not know exactly when the Valentinians began to separate from established churches and set up their own congregations. It is certain, however, that they did so, for at the end of the second century Clement speaks of them as a distinct Christian group with their own doctrines and rituals. On the latter question see also the destruction of a Valentinian meeting place by other Christians (c. 388) in Ambrose

Letters 62. The date of Clement's instruction by Pantaenus is based on Eus. *H.E.* 5.9.1–10.1; 11.1–2; 6.6.1. On Pantaenus as Clement's teacher see Eus. *H.E.* 5.11.1f.; on Pantaenus as the head of a Christian school in Alexandria see Eus. *H.E.* 5.10.1–4.

[10] On Clement's birth to pagan parents see Eus. *P.E.* 2.2.64; on his birth in Athens or Alexandria see Epiph. *Panar.* 1.2.32.6. The date of Clement's birth is conjectural and read back from the supposed time of his work in Alexandria. On the travels of Clement in search of instruction see *Strom.* 1.11.2 (2.8.20–2,4; 8.23–9.3); on Clement's probable conversion to Christianity see his own remarks in *Paed.* 1.1.1 (1.90.5f.); on Clement as head of the school see Eus. *H.E.* 6.6.1. See also Clement's flight from Alexandria during a persecution that occurred (c. 202–3) in the reign of Septimius Severus in Eus. *H.E.* 6.6.1; 1.1; 3.1; Clement bearing a letter to the church in Antioch (c. 211) on behalf of his former pupil Alexander, the bishop of a community in Cappadocia, in Eus. *H.E.* 6.11.5–6; 14.9; 11.1–2; Alexander mentioning Clement in the letter as a "blessed presbyter" whose work has strengthened and increased the church in Eus. *H.E.* 6.11.6; and Alexander's subsequent letter (c. 215–6) reporting the death of Clement in Eus. *H.E.* 6.14.9. On Demetrius as bishop of Alexandria see Eus. *H.E.* 5.22.1; 6.2.2; on Demetrius having control of the catechetical school see Eus. *H.E.* 6.3.2; 6.8.3; 5.10.1-3.

[11] On Clement's support of Demetrius see the remarks about bishops, presbyters, and deacons as leaders of the church in *Strom.* 6.107.2-3 (2.485.28-32); cf. *Strom.* 6.106.2-3 (2.485.10-7) where Clement infers that sometimes leaders in the church did not uphold the highest standards of Christian conduct. Note that very few of Clement's writings are extant. The most important works of his which still survive are the *Protrepticus, Paedagogus*, and *Stromateis*. Together, these treatises form a kind of trilogy in which the *Protrepticus* attempts to convert people to the Christian faith by demonstrating the errors of pagan religion and philosophy, the *Paedagogus* delineates the proper conduct for new converts by expounding the ethical teachings of Jesus, and the *Stromateis* outlines the true philosophy of the Christian religion by opposing the false doctrines of the Greek philosophers and certain heretics like Basilides, Valentinus, and their disciples. Other extant materials from the works of Clement include: the *Excerpta ex Theodoto*, a collection of notes on the teachings of Valentinians such as Theodotus and Ptolemy; the *Eclogae Propheticae,* a series of interpretive comments on the scripture; the *Quis Dives Salvetur?*, a homily on the proper use of wealth; and fragments of miscellaneous writings. With regard to the Greek text, I have used that of O. Stählin because it is the standard edition of Clement's writings. The only exception to this occurs when I employ the text of the *Excerpta ex Theodoto* given by F. Sagnard. The latter, however, is essentially the same as that of Stählin; see Sagnard, *Extraits de Théodote*, p. 50. Any changes in the text of Stählin are noted. In my translations, I also have placed quotation marks only around material that is identical with that printed in the best modern editions. This is done to show the reader how much Clement and his opponents altered the original material to fit a given context or how much the readings in their texts differed from those in ours.

1

The Basilideans and Valentinians
on the Origin of the World

Basilides and His Followers

IN two passages of the *Stromateis,* Clement of Alexandria relates how his predecessor Basilides thought that the world is one even though God is not and that two divine beings, named Righteousness and Peace, were placed in the eighth heaven where they remain. Although Clement does not reveal the source from which he took this information, he apparently knew, as did other writers, that Basilides believed in the existence of a supreme God living in a supermundane realm and a lower deity ruling over the created world. Basilides also envisioned the supreme God bringing forth other divine entities, like Righteousness and Peace, and placing them in various heavenly realms.[1]

Judging from Clement's remarks in another part of the *Stromateis,* both Basilides and his son Isidore taught that evil spirits inhabit the human soul and fill it with passions in accordance with their own nature. With an allusion to an image found in the writings of Plato, Basilides claims that there are as many spirits in the souls of human beings as there were soldiers in the Trojan horse. In his book, *On the Soul Attached to Us,* Isidore expresses agreement with this doctrine of his father by explaining how some people say that the evil spirits in their souls force them to commit evil deeds. Isidore, however, argues that such people only want to do what is wrong and make no effort to resist the force of the spirits. He concludes that all human beings must demonstrate control over the passions of their lower nature by strengthening the rational faculty in their souls.[2]

Like the founder of their movement, certain Basilideans maintained a dualistic theology by describing how the Ruler of the world became afraid when he learned about the existence of a superior power in the realm above him. In the second book of the *Stromateis* these followers of Basilides are quoted as saying:

> when the Ruler heard the statement of the ministering Spirit, he was terrified both by what was heard and seen since he was given the good news beyond his expectation; and his terror was called fear, which was the beginning of wisdom that is able to classify and distinguish and perfect and restore; for he who is over all sent it forth, distinguishing not only the world, but also the elect.[3]

The Basilideans explain in the passage above how the saying in the book of Proverbs: "The fear of God is the beginning of wisdom": means that the Ruler obtained wisdom when he was terrified by the sight and the sound of the ministering Spirit. Though they do not provide any explicit information about the identity of the Ruler or the ministering Spirit, the Basilideans seem to equate the former with the Ruler of the eighth or seventh heaven and the latter with the Holy Spirit, as in the *Refutation of All Heresies* by Hippolytus. If this is the case, the Ruler in the citation above became terrified when the Spirit told him the good news about the existence of the supermundane realm above him and when he saw the Spirit functioning as the boundary between that realm and the world below.

The good news about the transcendent realm exceeded the Ruler's expectation and terrified him because he had previously believed that nothing existed above him and that he alone was God. The Ruler's fear, therefore, was the beginning of wisdom, for he learned that a superior deity—the true God—existed above him. This good news about the supreme God was sent by the Holy Spirit to the Ruler so all things in creation might be classified into their respective kinds and be restored to their proper place, and the elect people in the world might eventually attain perfection. The Basilideans suggest that this process of classification, restoration, and perfection is part of a plan of salvation set in motion by the supreme deity. Through this plan, they, as the elect people, will be separated from the world of the Ruler and return to their place of origin in the supermundane realm. In a section of book four of the *Stromateis* certain Basilideans confirm the idea of a divine plan of salvation by saying that providence begins to be moved because of the Ruler.[4]

Elsewhere, in the second book of the *Stromateis*, some Basilideans are reported to have followed the teachings of Isidore and his father regarding the presence of spirits in the human soul. Referring to the passions of the soul as appendages, these Basilideans say:

> in essence they are certain spirits which were attached to the rational
> soul in accordance with an original confusion and disturbance; and
> again, other bastard and different natures of spirits, like that of a wolf,
> ape, lion, or goat, grow as an accretion upon them, whose attributes,
> appearing around the soul, make the desires of the soul exactly like
> those of the animals; for they imitate the actions of those whose
> attributes they bear; and not only do they have an affinity with the
> impulses and fantasies of irrational animals, but they imitate the
> movements and beauties of plants on account of bearing also the
> attributes of plants which are attached to them; and again, they even
> have the attributes of a state, like the hardness of steel.[5]

The followers of Basilides explain in the quotation above how the passions are actually appendages that became attached to the rational part of the human soul in the confusion of things that prevailed at the beginning of the world. Without explaining anything more about the creation, the Basilideans affirm that during life, the original spirits in the human soul are joined by other spirits that have natures like those of various plants, animals, and things. The original spirits then begin to produce passions in the soul resembling the nature of the new spirits that have become attached to them. Therefore, people are prompted to act in accordance with the passions that have been produced in their souls by the spirits. In a subsequent portion of the *Stromateis* the Basilideans contend that pain and fear are added to the soul like rust to iron.[6]

Valentinus

As in the case of the Basilideans, Clement provides his readers with material from the writings of Valentinus wherein aspects of the creation of the world are discussed. In a fragment cited in book four of the *Stromateis*, Valentinus declares:

> as much as the image is less than the living face, so much is the world less than the living Aeon. What, then, is the cause of the image? It is the majesty of the face that supplied the model to the painter so that it might be honored through his name; for a form was not discovered exactly, but the name filled the deficiency in the fashioned thing. And the invisibility of God also cooperates for the faith of that which has been fashioned.[7]

Valentinus argues in this fragment that the nature of the visible world is inferior to that of the divine world or Pleroma in the same way that a portrait is inferior to the living face which it depicts. In fact, like an artist, who honors a person by painting their portrait, Sophia gave honor to the Pleroma by creating the world in its image. Even though the world was not a perfect copy of the Pleroma, its deficiency was rectified when the name of God, that is, the Savior came down to redeem the human race. Valentinus concludes that the power of God exhibited by the Savior helps those who are in the world to become faithful and thus be saved.

The founder of the Valentinian movement also reflects on the creation of the human race in a fragment from one of his many letters. In the fragment, which is quoted in book two of the *Stromateis*, Valentinus says:

> and just as fear existed for the angels in the presence of that molded

form when it uttered sounds greater than its molding (because of the one who had invisibly deposited in it a seed of the substance from above and who spoke freely), so also among the races of earthly men the works of men became objects of fear for those who made them, as in the case of statues and images and everything which hands make in the name of a god. For Adam, who was molded in the name of "Man," supplied fear of the pre-existent Man, indeed, because he was established in him; and they were terrified and quickly hid their work.[8]

Valentinus describes in this fragment how the angels of the Demiurge created Adam in the image of the Aeon Man and became terrified and hid their creation when he began to speak after a spiritual element was placed in him. The angels were surprised by Adam's sudden ability to speak because they were unaware that a spiritual seed had been deposited in him by Sophia. Since the seed was of the same divine substance and power as the Aeon Man and the supreme deity in the Pleroma, Adam was able to speak and thus become an instrument for utterances from the divine world. The angels, however, were terrified by their creature because they knew that the power manifested in his speech could not have been produced by the psychic substance from which they had originally made him. In fact, the terror of the angels was like that of artisans who become afraid of the statues of the gods that they have made when those images seem to manifest divine power. Consequently, the angels attempted to hide Adam from the Pleroma by clothing his psychic and spiritual elements in a body of flesh. As Valentinus claims elsewhere in the *Stromateis*, the whole human race was sentenced to death when the Demiurge caused his angels to clothe the first man in a physical body that was subject to corruption. From the aforegoing statements, we can see how Valentinus, like the Basilideans, espoused a dualistic theology—one which posited a radical separation between the supreme God and the creator of the world.[9]

The Valentinians

Unfortunately, we do not know much more about the theology of Valentinus than that which Clement has preserved in the preceding fragments. In the fifth book of the *Stromateis*, though, Clement does make a passing remark about the theology of certain followers of Valentinus. There Clement describes how some Valentinians refer to the supreme God as "the Depth" and think that this deity comprehends and contains everything while not being comprehended or contained himself. The Valentinians who are quoted in the *Excerpta ex Theodoto* also say that a female entity, named Silence, coexisted with the Depth from the very beginning and was the mother of all the other divine beings who were created. Silence was aptly named because the nature of the Depth could not be expressed by her. She did, however, call the Depth "incomprehensible" since this was all that she could understand about him. According to the Valentinian Theodotus, the Father gave himself to Silence in spite of his unchanging nature so that she might understand something about his compassion.[10]

The disciples of Valentinus add to their description in the *Excerpta* by explaining how the supreme deity sought to make himself known to other beings. The Valentinians use some material from the Gospel of John to state:

> therefore, since the Father was unknown, he wished to become known to the Aeons; and through his own thought, as he knew himself, he put forth the Only-begotten as the Spirit of knowledge that is in knowledge. So, too, the one who came forth from knowledge, that is, from the thought of the Father, became knowledge, that is, the Son, because the Father was known through the Son. But the Spirit of love was mixed with the Spirit of knowledge, as the Father with the Son and thought with Truth, having come forth from the Truth as knowledge from thought. And the one who remained the "Only-begotten" Son "in the bosom of the Father" explained thought to the Aeons through knowledge as he also was put forth from his bosom.[11]

The same section of the *Excerpta* as above provides us with further information on the emanation of divine beings in the heavenly world. Interpreting the incipit of the Gospel of John, the Valentinians claim:

> "the Beginning" is the Only-begotten, who also is called God, as in the verses immediately following it shows that he is God when it says: "The Only-begotten God, who is in the bosom of the Father, he has declared him." The Logos that is "in the Beginning", that is, in the Only-begotten—in the Mind and the Truth—it indicates as the Christ—the Logos and the Life; whence it rightfully calls him God—the one who is in God, the Mind. "What came into being in him", the Logos, "was Life," the syzygy.[12]

The Valentinians show in these statements how the Father, who had existed from eternity as perfect mind, desired to make himself known to other beings because hitherto he had been known only to himself. Therefore, while absorbed in contemplating himself, the Father brought forth from the depths of his thought another being, who was identical in essence with him and who was called "the Only-begotten". Since the Only-begotten came forth from the thought of the Father, he was the Son of the Father, the very embodiment of the Father's knowledge of himself, and the only one who could reveal knowledge of the Father to other beings.   The Only-begotten Son or "beginning" also contained a host of other divine beings within himself, including the Truth, Logos, Life, and Christ.   As other Valentinian sources tell us, the Son subsequently brought forth from himself the Truth as his female companion and thereby created the male-female pair or Aeon—Son-Truth. Immediately afterwards, other Aeons such as Logos-Life, Man-Church, and Christ-Holy Spirit came forth in succession from each other.   Since the Son possessed the Spirit of love and that of knowledge, he told the rest of the Aeons about the Father's desire to become known to them.[13]

From several other passages in the *Excerpta*, we see how the Valentinians thought that the various Aeons were identical in essence with the Father and the Son.   Other emanations of Aeons continued in stages down to the twelfth and last one, Sophia, at which point the divine world consisted of thirty members. Each of the Aeons was complete in itself because it was joined with a male or female partner in an intellectual and eternal marriage.   Collectively, the Aeons or logoi comprised the All or Pleroma and thus expressed the fullness of the attributes of the unbegotten Father from whom they had come.[14]

Despite the fact that the Aeons were identical in essence with the Father, and reflected the manifold attributes of his being, each one was an individual in its own right and therefore distinct from the Father himself.   Indeed, the Aeons were arranged in a hierarchy of space and time that proceeded from the Son, who was the first Aeon to come forth and the one nearest the Father, down to the last Aeon to come forth and the one furthest from the Father, Sophia.   Since the Aeons were separated from the Father due to their emanation from him, and those who came forth last were furthest from the source of their being, a state of inequality existed among the divine entities and rendered them capable of taking individual action.   The inequality among the Aeons was shown by the fact that the Only-begotten Son had knowledge of the Father while the last Aeon, Sophia, did not.   Sophia's desire to obtain knowledge of the Father and her failure to do so eventually caused a breach in the unity and harmony of the divine world and started a series of events which culminated in the creation of the world outside the Pleroma.[15]

The followers of Valentinus describe the inordinate desire of Sophia and its negative effect on the Pleroma in a series of statements located near the middle of the *Excerpta*.   There the Valentinians say:

> moreover, when the passion took place, the whole itself also shared in suffering for the correction of the one who suffered.
>   ...But also, through the persuasion of the twelfth Aeon, the whole, having been educated, shared in suffering.
>   For then, they knew that what they are—a nameless name, form,

and knowledge—they are by the grace of the Father.

But the Aeon who wished to grasp that which is beyond knowledge fell into ignorance and lack of form; whence it also produced a void of knowledge, that is, a shadow of the name—the name that is the Son, the form of the Aeons. So the partial name of the Aeons was a loss of the name.[16]

The Valentinians discuss in the remarks above how Sophia, the twelfth and last Aeon, experienced a desire to comprehend the Father who was beyond knowledge, and in her passion to know him exhibited her ignorance of the fact that he was incomprehensible. Though the Valentinian material in the *Excerpta* does not explain the persuasion of Sophia in detail, other texts reveal how Sophia was convinced by a power called "Limit" that her attempt to comprehend the Father was impossible, and so she was healed of her passion and saved from being swallowed up in the depths of the Father's being.[17] The passionate quest of Sophia, however, caused the rest of the Aeons in the Pleroma to suffer, for it introduced desire, passion, and ignorance into a realm that previously had enjoyed perfection. Consequently, in their compassion for Sophia, the other Aeons requested that the Father dispel the ignorance of their sister who had suffered, whereupon the Son was given the task of instructing the whole Pleroma. As the only one who had knowledge of the Father, the Son was able to educate the other Aeons by revealing the name or knowledge of the supreme deity to them. Through this instruction the Aeons learned that they could not obtain full knowledge of the Father because his nature was incomprehensible, but that by his grace they had become a part of him. In this way the Aeons gained an understanding of their proper relationship to the Father and the original unity and harmony of the Pleroma was partially restored.

Though the Aeons in the Pleroma were instructed by the Son, Sophia's passionate desire to grasp the incomprehensible Father could not be simply undone. From sources outside the *Excerpta*, we learn that after the persuasion of Sophia, her passionate desire was separated from her and cast outside the Pleroma. There, in a void of darkness and ignorance the desire of the twelfth Aeon was hypostatized as another being—the lower Sophia. Created in the image of her mother, and possessing her mother's desire, the lower Sophia was prevented from reentering the Pleroma by the Limit, which defined the boundary between the divine world and the realm below it. Outside the Pleroma, the lower Sophia underwent the various passions of grief, fear, terror, and dismay that her mother had experienced before her.[18]

Theodotus and certain other Valentinians in the *Excerpta* explain that after she was excluded from the Pleroma, the lower Sophia brought forth the Christ from her thought and that this Christ was a complete being made in the image of the Father and the Aeons above him. According to the Valentinians, the

words in the book of Genesis: "he made them male and female": mean that
Christ was a complete being because he contained both the male and female
elements within himself. But the words: "he created" them "in the image of
God": refer to Christ being only a reflection of the things in the Pleroma since
he was put forth by Sophia alone rather than from a pair. In addition, the male
element in Christ was called "angelic" because it was the substance from which
the Savior and his male angels, the election, were soon to be created. On the
other hand, the female element in Christ was the "superior seed" or spiritual
substance that was to be placed in the souls of chosen human beings.[19]

The disciples of Valentinus make allusions to several passages in the New
Testament as they describe in more detail how Christ fled that which was
foreign to him and was drawn up into the Pleroma where he was mixed with the
Aeons and the Paraclete or Holy Spirit. Christ became a "son" of the Pleroma
because his male-female nature was identical with that of the Aeons, who were
"sons" of the Father; yet he was an "adopted son" in that he, unlike the Aeons,
had been put forth outside the Pleroma. Christ also became the "elect" by
virtue of his having the male, angelic element of the election and the "First-
born" by being the first to be born outside the Pleroma. So, too, the superior
seeds went with Christ into the Pleroma and were purified there in the divine
light. Since these seeds would later be placed in the souls of those people who
were called to be Christians, the church was said to have been chosen, gathered,
and manifested in the Pleroma before the creation of the world. Subsequently,
as other Valentinians in the *Excerpta* affirm, Christ requested that the Aeons
redress the situation of his mother who had been left outside, and with their
assistance he brought forth from his male substance the Savior to be a
comforter for the lower Sophia. Then the Savior himself brought forth a host
of angels from his own male substance and these angels became the male
counterparts of the female seeds.[20]

Resuming their narrative about the activities of the lower Sophia, the
Valentinians in the *Excerpta* show how she produced the future creator of the
world, the Demiurge, in her desire for the Christ who had left her. Sophia,
though, was disgusted when she saw the Demiurge because he was inferior to
the Christ in whose image he had been created. This inferiority was due to the
fact that the Demiurge was produced from Sophia's passionate desire and thus
was psychic in nature, whereas Christ had been created from Sophia's spiritual
substance and so was a spiritual being. After producing the Demiurge, Sophia
went on to create the material substance on the left and the psychic substance
on the right from her various passions. Later, Sophia formed psychic beings or
powers from the psychic substance, and the Demiurge created material beings
from the material substance. At this point, Sophia requested that the light of
Christ return to her whereupon the Savior was sent forth from the Pleroma.[21]

The Valentinians go on in the *Excerpta* to discuss the Savior's descent from the Pleroma with the aid of material drawn from a number of passages in the scripture. Theodotus and some of his disciples give one version of this event when they say:

> Jesus our light, as the apostle says, "having emptied himself"—that is, having passed outside the Limit—led out the angels of the superior seed with himself since he was an angel of the Pleroma; and he had redemption because he came forth from the Pleroma, but he led the angels for the correction of the seed; for inasmuch as they are bound and make entreaty on behalf of the parts and are held back on account of us, even though they hasten to enter, they beg remission for us in order that we might enter with them; for one might almost say that they have need of us so that they might enter; since it is not permitted for them to enter without us (for this reason even the mother has not gone in without us), they are naturally bound on behalf of us.[22]

In another section of the *Excerpta* certain Valentinians give a second rendition of the Savior's descent by quoting from the scripture and asserting:

> and when the Father gave all power, and the Pleroma also consented, the "angel of the counsel" is sent forth. And he becomes head of all things after the Father; for "all things were created by him", "things visible and invisible", "thrones", "dominions", kingdoms, divinities, and services; "therefore, God also exalted him and" gave "him a name that is above every name", "so that every knee might bend" "and every tongue confess that Jesus Christ", the Savior, "is the Lord" of glory. He who ascended also descended. "What does it mean to say that he ascended, except that he also descended?" "He who descended" "into the lower parts of the earth" "is the same one who also ascended above the heavens".[23]

The comments of the Valentinians in the aforegoing passages portray the unbegotten Father and the Aeons giving all power to Jesus the Savior and sending him beyond the boundary of the Pleroma to be the light and angel of counsel for the lower Sophia. As he went out from the Pleroma, the Savior became the head of everything after the Father because all things visible and invisible were eventually to be created by him. He also received all of the spiritual power of the Pleroma so he would be recognized as an emissary of the Father and a manifestation of the divine world. The descent of the Savior into the realm of the void and shadow was only temporary, however, for he was destined to return to the Pleroma with Sophia at the end of time. Although the Savior did not need to be redeemed, since he had been brought forth by Christ in the Pleroma, he led his male angels outside the Limit to redeem the superior seeds. As the female counterparts of the male angels, the superior seeds were soon to placed in the souls of chosen human beings. The redemption of the seeds was necessary because the angels and Sophia were not able to reenter the Pleroma without them.

The Valentinians add to their narrative in the *Excerpta* by explaining how Sophia worshipped the Savior when she recognized that he was like the Christ who had left her, but hid herself behind a veil in shame at the sight of the male angels. In fact, Sophia putting on a veil in the presence of the male angels later became the basis for the apostle Paul's command that women wear a veil during worship in the church.[24] After Sophia's response to his appearance, the Savior taught the woman outside the Pleroma about the emanation of the Aeons from the Father and the other events that led to her expulsion from the heavenly world. Through the revelation of this knowledge Sophia was relieved of the passions that had originated from her ignorance about the Father, and thereby, she became impassible.[25]

Proceeding to an account of the further activities of the Savior, the Valentinians in the *Excerpta* describe the creation of the material and psychic elements from which certain things in the visible world were destined to be made. The Valentinians quote a passage from the Gospel of John to say:

> ...and the passions were not carried away as the things of the one within, but he led both them and the things of the second disposition into substance. Thus Sophia became impassible through the appearance of the Savior, and the things outside were created. For "all things were made through him, and without him was not anything made".
>
> First, therefore, he drew them from incorporeal and accidental passion and transformed them into matter still incorporeal, then, in this way, into compounds and bodies; for it was not possible to bring the passions into substance at once; and he placed properties in the bodies in accordance with their nature.
>
> Therefore, the Savior became the first universal creator.[26]

With these discrete remarks the Valentinians claim that the Savior transformed the passions of the lower Sophia into an incorporeal substance because they could not be simply cast away as had those of her mother in the Pleroma. The Savior also transformed into an incorporeal substance Sophia's second disposition, which had come into being when she underwent a conversion and requested that the light of Christ return to her. First, the Savior transformed the passions and second disposition of Sophia into incorporeal matter, and then into compounds and bodies, which he endowed with properties suitable to their nature. These two stages of transformation were necessary because the passions and second disposition could not be simply changed into substances by a single process. Thus the Savior was able to bring into being a material element from the passions of Sophia and a psychic element from her conversion. From these two elements, the Savior prepared to create the material and psychic beings outside the Pleroma and so become the first universal creator.

In a different section of the *Excerpta* the Valentinians assert that at some point after the Savior appeared to her, Sophia gave birth to the superior seeds. The Valentinians say:

> the mother, who brought forth the Christ complete and was left behind by him, no longer put forth anything complete in the future, but held back what was possible by herself; so that, having put forth the angelic elements of both Place and the called, she keeps them by herself, since the angelic elements of the elect had been put forth still earlier by the male.
>
> For, on the one hand, those on the right were brought forth by the mother before her request for the light, but the seeds of the church after her request for the light, when the angelic elements of the seeds were put forth by the male.

Immediately following the preceding passage, the Valentinian teacher Theodotus also remarks:

> the superior seeds neither came forth as passions (for when they are destroyed, the seeds also would be dissolved with them), nor as a creation (for when the creation is brought to completion, the seeds also would be completed with it), but as children; wherefore it also has an affinity with the light, that is, Jesus, whom Christ first brought forth when he asked the Aeons.[27]

Here, through a series of doctrinal statements, the Valentinians say that Sophia no longer brought forth anything with a male and female substance after Christ had abandoned her. Instead, Sophia put forth the superior seeds as incomplete and formless elements when she saw the Savior and his angels following her request for the return of Christ. These superior seeds were "angelic elements of both Place and the called" because they were produced under the influence of the male angels in the midst of the dwelling place of the psychic Demiurge, who, later, would be called to salvation. Theodotus also insists that the superior seeds did not come forth as passions, like the psychic element, or as something which had been created, like the material element;

rather they came forth as children who are spiritual in nature, like Sophia, the Savior, and the Pleroma. In spite of their spiritual nature, however, the seeds were destined to enter the material world in order to be educated and healed, for presently they still were the weak and ignorant children of Sophia.[28]

Having detailed the manner in which the spiritual, psychic, and material elements came into being outside the Pleroma, the Valentinians in the *Excerpta* give an interesting description of how Sophia became a second creator after the Savior. The Valentinians say:

> ...but "Sophia", the second, "built a house for herself and hewed out seven pillars". And, first of all, she put forth a god as an image of the Father, and through him, she made "the heavens and the earth," that is, "the heavenly things and the earthly things"—the things on the right and the left. As an image of the Father, this one became a father and first put forth the psychic Christ as an image of the Son, then the archangels as images of the Aeons, then the angels of the archangels. These were from the psychic and luminous substance, about which the prophetic word says: "And the Spirit of God was borne above the waters", expressing how, in the combination of the two substances made by him, the pure was borne above, but the heavy and material— the turbid and gross—was borne underneath. But by saying "invisible" it is even suggested that this was incorporeal in the beginning; for neither was it invisible to man, who was not yet created, nor to God, because he made it; but in some way the saying affirmed the lack of form and shape and figure of it.
>
> And, separating the pure things from the heavy, as he saw the nature of each one, the Demiurge made light, that is, he made manifest and introduced them both into light and form, since he made the light of the sun and heaven much later; and he made one of the material elements from grief, creating in essence the evil spirits, "against whom we must fight"; wherefore the apostle also says: "And do not grieve the Holy Spirit of God, in whom you were sealed". He also made the wild beasts from fear and the elements of the world from terror and dismay. And in the three elements the fire floats and is disseminated and hides and is kindled by them and dies with them because it has no appointed place of its own like the other elements from which the compound substances are fashioned.[29]

The Valentinians interpret a number of scriptural texts in this account to depict Sophia creating the Demiurge in imitation of the Father and through him making a host of psychic beings on the right and material beings on the left. Acting under the direction of Sophia without being aware of it, the Demiurge separated the psychic and material substances whereupon the more pure, psychic substance floated to an intermediate position below the Pleroma while the grosser, material element was borne down to the lowest part of the universe. Then, from the psychic substance, the Demiurge created the psychic Christ, archangels, and angels respectively in imitation of the Son, Aeons, and male angels. The Demiurge and the first beings created by him were actually inferior to those in whose image they were fashioned because they were psychic rather than spiritual in nature. The Demiurge went on to create evil spirits, demons, and the three elements of earth, water, and air from the material substance that had been made from Sophia's passions of grief, fear, terror, and dismay. Within the three elements, though, there was hidden a fourth element of fire. This fire was not only kindled by the other elements, but destined to destroy them and itself at the end of time.

A little further on, in the same section of the *Excerpta*, the Valentinians resume their description of the Demiurge by explaining how he thought that he alone was responsible for his creative activity. The Valentinians say:

> since he did not know the one who operated through him, he supposed that he created by his own power, being industrious by nature. On account of this, the apostle said: He "was subject to the vanity" of the world, "not willingly, but on account of the one who subjected" him, "in the hope that" he "also shall be set free" when the seeds of God are brought together. And a particular proof of his involuntary action is the fact that he blessed the Sabbath and was exceedingly fond of rest from his labors.[30]

Material from Romans and Genesis is interpreted by the Valentinians in the passage above to assert that Sophia used the Demiurge as an unwitting agent to create the visible world in the image of the Pleroma and thus bring about the ultimate salvation of the superior seeds. The Valentinian portrayal of the ignorant Demiurge here is a direct attack on the deity of the Jewish scriptures because it states that the creator of the world was subject to the power of the true God, the unbegotten Father, and those acting on his behalf, such as the Savior and Sophia. The description of the Demiurge in this text is not as openly hostile as that in other Gnostic tracts like the *Apocryphon of John* or *Hypostasis of the Archons* and may reflect a Valentinian effort to modify earlier traditions in response to the polemics of ecclesiastical opponents. In any case, the Valentinians assert that the Demiurge was ignorant of the existence of his mother and the Pleroma, powerless to act by himself, and perverse by nature. The perversity of the Demiurge was exhibited by the fact that he preferred to rest rather than work and even went so far as to bless the Sabbath on which he ceased from his creative activity.

Discussing the subsequent events of the creation, the Valentinians in the *Excerpta* draw upon several passages in Genesis to describe how the Demiurge made the first human being. According to them, the Demiurge created the first member of the human race in light of the idea of man that he possessed before making the elements of the visible world. The Demiurge took "dust from the earth" or incorporeal matter to fashion an invisible, material soul "according to" his own "image". This material soul was irrational, full of passion, and identical in essence with the nature of the wild beasts because it was made from the material substance that had been derived from the passions of Sophia. Next, the Demiurge created a psychic soul "according to" his own "likeness" by using his angels to breathe some of the psychic substance into the material soul of the man. At this point the Demiurge referred to the psychic soul as the "breath of life" since the man was still incorporeal; but later, he called it a "living soul" when the man was fully formed.[31]

The followers of Valentinus elaborate on the creative work of the Demiurge by explaining that the psychic and material souls were joined together as a whole through inexpressible power. Therefore, the statement in Genesis: "This now is bone of my bones": indicates that the psychic soul was firm, impassive, and strong, and that it was hidden in the material soul as a bone is hidden in the flesh of human beings. Likewise, the phrase "flesh of my flesh" in the same text suggests that the material soul functioned as the body of the psychic soul. The Valentinians conclude that the Demiurge must have created these aspects of the first man in the fourth heaven or Paradise since it is impossible for any physical body to be in that realm.[32]

After completing their narrative concerning the creation of the psychic and material souls, the Valentinians claim that Sophia placed a spiritual seed inside the first man. With a quote from Galatians they say:

> and without his knowledge Adam had the spiritual seed sown into his soul by Sophia—"established", he says, "through angels by the hand of a mediator; and the mediator is not one; but God is one." Therefore, the seeds that were put forth into generation by Sophia are ministered to by the male angels, wherefore it was possible for them to come into being. For, just as the Demiurge, who is secretly moved by Sophia, thinks that he is self-moved, so also do men. Therefore, Sophia first put forth the spiritual seed in Adam, so that the bone—the rational and heavenly soul—might not be empty, but be full of spiritual marrow.[33]

Near the beginning of the *Excerpta*, the Valentinians complement the aforegoing description of the insemination of the first man by stating:

> when the psychic body was formed, a male seed (which is an effluence

of the angelic) was placed by the Logos in the elect soul while it was asleep so that there might not be a deficiency. And this acted as leaven to unite the soul and the flesh, which appeared to be divided and which had been put forth separately by Sophia; and the sleep for Adam was the forgetfulness of the soul, which the spiritual seed—the one that the Savior placed in the soul—held together in order that it might not be divided. The seed was an effluence of the male and angelic.[34]

The Valentinians contend in these two reports that the Savior prompted Sophia to sow a superior seed into the psychic soul of Adam without the man being aware of it. From other sources, we learn that the male angels secretly deposited the seed in the Demiurge without his knowledge and that the seed was sown into the material soul of Adam along with the psychic substance. Later, the male angels employed the same method to put a spiritual seed into the souls of all human beings who were chosen for salvation. Indeed, it was necessary for such people to receive the spiritual seed so the rational and divine element within them—the soul—might be filled with spiritual power like a bone filled with marrow. Otherwise, just as the Demiurge, all human beings would remain ignorant of the spiritual realm and think that they acted of their own free will.

The seed that was sown into the psychic soul of Adam was called "male" since it was brought forth by Sophia in the likeness of the male angels and was of the same spiritual substance as them. The seed also acted as leaven to unite the psychic and material souls because these two souls had been created separately by Sophia and thus appeared to be divided. In fact, the spiritual seed strengthened the psychic soul to prevent it from being kept in a state of ignorance and being eventually destroyed by the material soul. Finally, even though the male aspect of the seed remained in Adam, the female aspect was taken from him and used to create the first woman, Eve.[35]

Alluding to part of the creation account in the book of Genesis, the Valentinians in the *Excerpta* relate how the first man was given a body of flesh. The Valentinians claim:

over the three incorporeal elements a fourth element, the earthy, was placed on Adam as the garments of skin. Therefore, Adam sows neither from the Spirit nor from that which was breathed into him; for both are divine and both are put forth through him, but not by him; and his material element is productive in seed and generation because it is mixed together with the seed, and it cannot stand aloof from this principle of union in life. In this sense, our father Adam is "the first man of the earth, earthy". But if he had sown both from the psychic and the spiritual as well as from the material, all would have been born equal and righteous, and the teaching would have been in all. On account of this, many are material, not many are psychic, and few are spiritual.[36]

The terse statements made by the Valentinians in the passage above endeavor to show how the Demiurge covered the material, psychic, and spiritual elements of Adam with a body of flesh fashioned from an earthy substance. Since this fleshly body prevented Adam from passing his psychic and spiritual elements on to his descendants, Sophia and the Demiurge transmitted these elements through the first man, but not by him. The material element of Adam, however, produced the seed of generation because it could not resist the impulse to procreate, and thereby the continuation of the human race was ensured so that all of the spiritual seeds might be brought into the world. If Adam had been able to sow from his psychic element, then all of his descendants would have possessed that element and would have been righteous. But if Adam had sown from his spiritual element, then all of his descendants would have received a spiritual seed and knowledge of the unbegotten Father. By virtue of his ability to sow only from his material element, there were many material, few psychic, and very few spiritual people among Adam's descendants.

The followers of Valentinus round out their anthropogony with a brief account of how three sons were begotten from the material, psychic, and spiritual elements of Adam. The first of these sons was the irrational man Cain, who was begotten from the material element in the image of the Demiurge. The second was the rational and just man Abel, who was begotten from the psychic element in the likeness of the Demiurge. The third son was the spiritual man Seth, who possessed the spiritual element that was identical in essence with Sophia, the Savior, and the Pleroma. Accordingly, the saying in Genesis: "This is the book of the generation of men": indicates that three races came into being among the subsequent generations of humankind and that each of these races had the same nature as its respective ancestor, Cain, Abel, or Seth. Of the three progenitors, only Seth bore fruit because his descendants were spiritual in nature. Furthermore, the descendants of Seth were destined to escape from the material world, for they recognized that their true home was in the Pleroma, and therefore, called upon the name of the Father.[37]

The Valentinians in the *Excerpta* bring their discussion of the origin of humankind to a close by describing the power of fate gaining control over everyone born into the material world. The Valentinians say:

fate is a union of many and opposing powers, and these are invisible and unseen, ruling the course of the stars and governing through them. For, in so far as each of them arrived, being carried along with the movement of the world, it obtained mastery over those who were born at that very moment, as if they were its children.

Therefore, through the fixed stars and planets, the invisible powers riding upon them control births and look upon them; yet the stars (τὰ ἄστρα) themselves do nothing (οὐδὲν ποιεῖ) but (δὲ) show the activity (τὴν ἐνέργειαν) of the ruling powers; just as a flight of birds also indicates (σημαίνει) something, but produces nothing.

So the twelve signs of the zodiac and the seven stars following them are sometimes in conjunction, sometimes in opposition, rising, falling, ... These show the movement of substance into the birth of living things and the turn of circumstances when they are moved by the powers. And both the stars and the powers are of different kinds—beneficent or maleficent, right or left—whose conjunction produces what is born; and through them each one comes into being at its own time, when the dominant sign accomplishes things in accordance with nature, partly at the beginning, partly at the end.

The Lord rescues us from this discord and battle of the powers and supplies peace from the conspiracy of the powers and the angels, some of whom are drawn up in battle order for us and others against us. For some are like soldiers who fight with us as servants of God, but others are like robbers; for the evil one did not live by the side of the king when he took up the sword, but out of madness seized for himself.

Indeed, on account of the adversaries, who occupy the soul and pledge it to slavery through the body and external things, those on the right are not sufficient to save and guard us as they follow us. For they are not perfectly providential like the good shepherd; but each one is like a hired hand, who sees the wolf approaching and flees and is unwilling to give up his life on behalf of his own sheep. And besides, since man, on behalf of whom the battle is fought, is also a weak animal, he is inclined toward the worse and helps those who hate him; whence even greater evils befall him.[38]

Through these remarks the Valentinians explain how the power of fate came into being when the Devil and other evil spirits attempted to seize control of the human race in opposition to the Savior and the good angels of the Demiurge. Due to this conflict, each of the good angels and evil spirits was able to acquire control over one of the planets or fixed stars of the zodiac. Subsequently, when a particular planet or star reached a dominant position in the heavens as it was carried around by the movement of the world, the good or evil power that ruled over that heavenly body managed to gain control of the life of any person who was being born at that time. The Valentinians insist that the stars and planets themselves did not have the power to cause anything. Instead, they simply displayed the activity of the various powers by indicating the birth and the circumstances in the lives of human beings. Thus everyone who was born into the world came under the influence of one of the spirits or angels, who, collectively, comprised the power of fate.

Although the angels of the Demiurge attempted to fight on behalf of the human race as servants of God, they were finally overcome by the Devil and the evil spirits, who attacked the souls of people like a band of robbers. The angels of the Demiurge were defeated in part because they fled from the evil spirits in order to save themselves, and therefore, did not exercise perfect care for the human beings as did the Savior. In time the evil spirits were able to occupy and control the soul of every person in the world. The task of the demons was made even easier by human beings, who were naturally weak on account of their material bodies and attachment to the things of the world. In fact, by following their natural inclination to do what was wrong, people helped the evil spirits obtain even greater control over their souls. At this point, only the Savior was capable of rescuing people and giving them peace from the unequal battle between the powers.

Finally, the Valentinians in the *Excerpta* describe how every person who died before the coming of the Savior was held in the realm of the Demiurge. Those who were psychic in nature and who had lived justly, as well as those who were spiritual in nature, were detained by the Demiurge in the seventh heaven after their material bodies died. Those who were material in nature, and those who were psychic in nature but who had lived unjustly, were kept among the demons on the left where they felt the fire that flowed out from under the throne of the Demiurge. As a principle of destruction, this fire flowed continuously into the world and fed the fire that was hidden in the three elements, thereby laying the foundation for the material world to be consumed at the end of time. Since the Demiurge himself had a fiery nature, only his son, the psychic Christ, could come before him without being destroyed— something which the Jewish high priest symbolized each year as he entered the Holy of Holies on the Day of Atonement. According to Theodotus, the Demiurge wore a veil so that the spiritual seeds detained by him would not be consumed by seeing his face. These seeds were members of the spiritual race, and they were destined to go up to the eighth heaven after the Savior sat down with the Demiurge and subdued him.[39]

Notes

[1] *Strom.* 5.74.3–4 (2.376.2–5); 4.162.1 (2.320.2ff.); cf. Iren. *Adv. Haer.* 1.24.3–4, 7; Hipp. *Refut.* 7.21.1f.; 23.3f.. On the relationship of the second fragment here to the account of Basilides' system in Irenaeus and the Valentinian Aeons see Grant, "Place de Basilide dans la théologie chrétienne ancienne," *Revue des études augustiniennes* 25 (1976) 209f.; Layton, *The Gnostic Scriptures*, pp. 428f..

[2] *Strom.* 2.113.2-114.2 (2.174.18–30). On the comparison of the soul to the Trojan horse see Plato *Theat.* 184d.

[3] *Strom.* 2.36.1–2 (2.131.30–32.6). On the "fear of God" as the beginning of wisdom see Prov. 1.7; on the Demiurge's fear of what is above him see also NHC II, 1, 14, 23–15, 13. On the relationship between the Basilidean material in the *Stromateis* and that in Hippolytus see Grant, "Place de Basilide dans la théologie chrétienne ancienne," *Revue des études augustiniennes* 25 (1979) 201f.. On the two Rulers and their domains see Hipp. *Refut.* 7.23.3–7; on the identity of the Spirit see Hipp. *Refut.* 7.23.1–2; on the two Rulers receiving the gospel see Hipp. *Refut.* 7.25.5–26.5; on the Spirit as the boundary between the supermundane world and the realm of the Ruler see Hipp. *Refut.* 7.23.1–2; on the reason for the Ruler's terror when he received the gospel see Hipp. *Refut.* 7.26.1–4; on the supreme God in the supermundane realm see Hipp. *Refut.* 7.20.2–21.1; on the sending of the gospel see Hipp. *Refut.* 7.25.5–7; on the distinction and classification of things see Hipp. *Refut.* 7.27.8–12; on the perfection of the elect see Hipp. *Refut.* 7.25.1–2; on the restoration of all things see Hipp. *Refut.* 7.27.1–4; on the restoration of the elect to the supermundane world see Hipp. *Refut.* 7.26.10; on the origin of the elect in the supermundane world see Hipp. *Refut.* 7.22.6–7, 16. See also *Exc.* 16 where the Basilideans appear to identify the Holy Spirit that enlightened the Ruler with the dove that descended upon Jesus; cf. Mark 1.9f.; Matt. 3.13f.; Luke 3.21f.; John 1.29f.. Note that all of my citations from the *Excerpta* follow the simple system of enumeration in the edition of Sagnard.

[4] *Strom.* 4.88.3 (2.287.1ff.); cf. Hipp. *Refut.* 7.25.5-26.5. See Foerster, "Das System des Basilides," *New Testament Studies* vol. 9, April 1963, no. 3, pp. 246f. where it is noted that the idea of providence in this passage "pabt genau zu dem System, das Hippolyt bietet."

[5] *Strom.* 2.112.1-113.1 (2.174.6–16). On the confusion of things see Hipp. *Refut.* 7.21.1f.; 27.8f..

[6] *Strom.* 4.88.5 (2.287.6–8).

[7] *Strom.* 4.89.6–90.3 (2.287.21–88.1). On the visible or material world being created in the image of the Pleroma and thus being inferior to its archetype see *Exc.* 47.2f.; on Sophia as a creator see *Exc.* 47.1; on the superior nature of the Pleroma causing Sophia to create see *Exc.* 33.3–4; 47.1–2; on the deficiency being filled when the Savior came as the name or knowledge of the Father see *Exc.* 43.2, 4; 22.7.

[8] *Strom.* 2.36.2–4 (2.132.6–16). On the angels of the Demiurge see *Exc.* 47.3; on the Demiurge and his angels creating man in the image of the pre-existing Man see NHC II, 1, 14, 13f.; on the Aeon Man in the divine world see Iren. *Adv. Haer.* 1.11.1; on the spiritual substance and the mother in Valentinus's doctrine see Iren. *Adv. Haer.* 1.11.1; on the connection between the Son and speech see *Strom.* 2.114.3–6 (2.174.31–75.14); on Adam being created from the psychic substance

see *Exc.* 50.2f.; on Adam being clothed in the fleshly body see *Exc.* 55.1; NHC II, 1, 20, 28–21, 16.

[9] *Strom.* 4.89.4–5 (2.287.16, 18ff.); on "no one shall see the face of God" see Ex. 33.20.

[10] *Strom.* 5.81.3–4 (2.380. 12ff.); cf. John 1.18; *Exc.* 29; 30.1. Note that Βυθός ("Depth") in *Strom.* 5.81.3-4 = Βάθος in *Exc.* 29. On the philosophical background of the incomprehensible and inexpressible First Principle see Festugière, "Notes sur les extraits de Théodote de Clement d'Alexandrie et sur les fragments d'Valentin," *Vigiliae Christianae* 3 (1949) 196ff.. The Depth and Silence are male and female aspects of a unified pair or syzygy. They complement each other and together express the unity, completeness, and perfection of the First Principle. As Sagnard remarks in *Extraits de Théodote*, p. 123 n.1: "Silence est la compagne normale (σύζυγος) de l'Abîme et contribue á marquer sa transcendance, son incognoscibilitié." On the Valentinian use of the names "Father" or "unbegotten Father" for the supreme God see also *Exc.* 47.2; 45.1; 64.

[11] *Exc.* 7.1-3. On the Father being made known through the Son see Matt. 11.27; Luke 10.22; John 1.18; on the "Only-begotten" and "in the bosom of the Father" see John 1.18.

[12] *Exc.* 6.1–4. On the first quote see John 1.1; on "the Only-begotten God..." see John 1.18; on the Logos "in the Beginning" see John 1.1f.; on the Life in the Logos see John 1.4; on the Logos as Christ see John 1.17; on "what came into being in him" see John 1.3f..

[13] On the constituent elements of the divine realm in the system of Valentinus see Irenaeus *Adv. Haer.* 1.11.1f.; for that of Ptolemy see Iren. *Adv. Haer.* 1.8.5f.. Both of these are similar to the system in *Exc.* 6.1f.. Note that it is only later, after the fall of Sophia, that the pair Christ-Holy Spirit is put forth in the Ptolemaic scheme shown in Iren. *Adv. Haer.* 1.2.5.

[14] *Exc.* 31.2; 32.1; 64; 25.1; 30.2; 22.4. On Sophia as the last Aeon see Iren. *Adv. Haer.* 1.2.2; on the thirty Aeons of the Pleroma see Iren. *Adv. Haer.* 1.1.1f.. These Aeons include the Ogdoad (8 Aeons), Decad (10 Aeons) and Duodecad (12 Aeons). The Aeons are "intellectual" (νοεροί) because they belong to the intelligible or spiritual world and "eternal" (αἰώνιοί) because they are divine. Each has its own "fullness" (πλήρωμα) because it constitutes a whole in union with its male or female companion. On the spiritual nature of the emanation and marriage of the Aeons see Clement's remark in *Strom.* 3.29.3 (2.209.26–9). The "Fullness" (τὸ Πλήρωμα) as a collective designation for the Aeons indicates the completeness of the divine world and its source, the unbegotten Father.

[15] The hierarchical organization of the Pleroma is indicated in *Exc.* 45.1: "the things as far as her" (τὰ μέχρι αὐτῆς). On knowledge of the Father and Sophia's desire see *Exc.* 7.1, 3; 31.3.

[16] *Exc.* 30.2; 31.2-4; cf. NHC I, 3, 38, 7; Iren. *Adv. Haer.* 1.2.2. It is said in Iren. *Adv. Haer.* 1.2.5 that the Aeons were instructed by Christ, who was put forth by the Only-begotten Son for this purpose; but in *Exc.* 32.2f. Christ is put forth outside the Pleroma after the education of the Aeons. In *Exc.* 31.2–3 then, the Aeons must have been instructed by the Only-begotten Son, unless this section comes from a different source than *Exc.* 32–33.

[17] See the various accounts in Iren. *Adv. Haer.* 1.2.1-6; Hipp. *Refut.* 6.29.5-32.1.

[18] On the desire and passion of Sophia being cast out of the Pleroma see Iren. *Adv. Haer.* 1.2.4; on Sophia outside the Pleroma see *Exc.* 23.2; on Sophia and Christ in the *Excerpta* see also Stead, "The Valentinian Myth of Sophia," *Journal of Theological Studies*, n.s., 20 (1960) 84ff.; on the Limit see *Exc.* 42.1; on the passions of the lower Sophia see Iren. *Adv. Haer.* 1.4.1–2; *Exc.* 48.2–3. Note that in the *Excerpta*, Sophia does not receive instruction in the Pleroma from Christ because the latter has not yet been brought forth.

[19] *Exc.* 32.2; 33.3; 39; 32.1; 21.1. Christ is "complete" because he possesses both the male and female elements. The same principle in *Exc.* 32.1 regarding that which comes from a pair or one appears in a fragment of Valentinus in *Strom.* 4.90.2–3 (2.287.30–88.1). On the creation of the male and female see Gen. 1.27. Note that the Valentinian text here replaces "him" (αὐτόν) in Gen. 1.27 with "them" (αὐτούς); on this point see also Sagnard, *Extr. de Théod.*, pp. 99 n.1; 133 n.3. On the emanation of the Savior and his male angels see *Exc.* 23.1f.; 39–40; on the female seed being placed within the souls of human beings see *Exc.* 53.2f..

[20] *Exc.* 33.3; 32.3–33.1; 41.2; 23.2; 39–40. On Christ as "elect" see Luke 9.35; 23.35; on Christ as the "First-born" see Col. 1.15; on the church being chosen before the creation of the world see Eph. 1.4; on the Paraclete see John 14.16; 1 John 2.1. The Paraclete in *Exc.* 32.3 is probably a reference to the Holy Spirit in the ordinary Christian sense since it is identified with Jesus in *Exc.* 23.1; on this point see Sagnard, *La Gnose valentinienne et le témoignage de Saint Irénée*, p. 541; *Extr. de Théod.*, p. 131 n.2.

[21] *Exc.* 33.3–34.1; 40. On the origin of the material and psychic substances from various passions of Sophia see also Iren. *Adv. Haer.* 1.4.1f..

[22] *Exc.* 35.1-4. On Jesus as the light see John 1.4f.; 8.12; on the Savior emptying himself see Phil. 2.7. The Savior possessed redemption because he was not put forth outside the Pleroma like Christ.

[23] *Exc.* 43.2–5. On the "angel of the counsel" see Is. 4.5; on "all things were created by him" see Col. 1.16. This section beginning with *Exc.* 43.2 and continuing until *Exc.* 65 is parallel to Iren. *Adv. Haer.* 1.4.5f., as several commentators have noted; on this question see Casey, *Exc. ex Theod.*, p. 22; Sagnard, *Extr. de Théod.*, pp. 28; 152 n.1; Foerster, *Gnosis*, vol. 1, p. 146. On "therefore God also exalted him" see Phil. 2.9ff.; on the quotations here concerning the one who ascended and descended see Eph. 4.9f..

[24] *Exc.* 44.1–2; see 1 Cor. 11.10.

[25] *Exc.* 45.1–2.

[26] *Exc.* 45.2–47.1. On "all things were made through him" see John 1.3.

[27] *Exc.* 39–40; 41.1–2. On the identification of the angelic elements of Place and the called with the female seeds see Sagnard, *Extr. de Théod.*, p. 143 n.5. It is necessary to maintain that the female seeds returned to Sophia after going up to the Pleroma with Christ, but how this happened and how the seeds became separated from the male substance with which they were originally put forth remains a mystery. See the discussion in Sagnard, *La Gnose Valent.*, pp. 555f. on this problem. The seeds are spiritual in nature (*Exc.* 53.2, 5), portions of the male angels with whom they have original and final unity (*Exc.* 22.1, 3; 35.3–36.2), and the divine particle of light in the soul of each Valentinian (*Exc.* 3.1–2; 58.1). The terms "the calling" (ἡ κλῆσις) or "the called" (τὸ κλητόν) and "the election" (ἡ ἐκλογή) or

"the elect" (τὸ ἐκλεκτόν) are relative. For example, in *Exc.* 21.1 the female elements are referred to as "the calling" in relation to the male elements or "the election" whereas in *Exc.* 58.1 the female seeds are referred to as "the elect" in relation to "the called" or psychic element.

[28] *Exc.* 68; 67.4; 79.

[29] *Exc.* 47.1-48.4. On Sophia building a house for herself see Prov. 9.1; on "the heavens and the earth" see Gen. 1.1; on the Spirit of God see Gen. 1.2; on "against whom we must fight" see Eph. 6.12; on "do not grieve the Holy Spirit of God" see Eph. 4.30. The Demiurge is "a god" in a derivative sense because he is an image of the true God, the unbegotten Father; cf. *Strom.* 4.90.2 (2.287.27ff.). The Demiurge also is called an "image of the Only-begotten" in *Exc.* 7.5 to indicate his inferiority to the Son. The principle underlying this description of the Demiurge and his creation is that any image is necessarily inferior to the object which it portrays. Hence the psychic Demiurge, Christ, archangels, and angels are inferior respectively to the spiritual Father, Son, Christ, and Aeons in the Pleroma; cf. *Strom.* 4.90.3–4 (2.288.4–7). Note that the Valentinians interpret the light in Gen. 1.3 as a reference to the elements being given form because, according to Gen. 1.16–9, the sun is made later, on the fourth day. With respect to the evil spirits, the Valentinians explain in a subsequent passage how the demons occupy the souls of human beings and control them through the power of fate; *Exc.* 69.1-73.3. People are only able to liberate themselves from the demons by receiving the Holy Spirit through baptism; *Exc.* 76.1-85.3. Thus Eph. 4.30 is interpreted here as an admonition for people to not continue living in a passionate manner after they have been sealed by the Holy Spirit.

[30] *Exc.* 49.1-2; cf. Rom. 8.20f.; Gen. 2.3. Note that the Valentinians have eliminated the phrase "the creation" (ἡ κτίσις) in Rom. 8.20 and replaced the phrase "the creation itself" (αὐτὴ ἡ κτίσις) in Rom. 8.21 with "he" (αὐτός), that is, the Demiurge. Unlike Paul, the Valentinians here thought that the creation was evil and destined for destruction and that the Demiurge was not the true God even though he was capable of being saved.

[31] *Exc.* 41.4; 50.1-3. On "dust from the earth" see Gen. 2.7; on the man "according to" the "image" and "likeness" see Gen. 1.26; on the "breath of life" and "living soul" see Gen. 2.7.

[32] *Exc.* 51.1-2. On "bone of my bones" and "flesh of my flesh" see Gen. 2.23. Contrary to the interpretation of Casey in *Exc. ex Theod.*, pp. 144f., the bone is the psychic soul and the flesh is the material soul. See also Foerster, *Von Valentin zu Herakleon*, p. 80 where it is stated that the breath blown into men by the Demiurge is the living, divine, heavenly, rational, and just soul.

[33] *Exc.* 53.2-5. On the quotation see Gal. 3.19f.. Here the seed is sown into Adam by Sophia while in *Exc.* 2.1-2 it is sown into Adam by the Logos-Savior. Apparently, the Valentinians thought that Sophia and the Logos-Savior acted in concert or the account in *Exc.* 53.2 relies upon a different tradition than that used in *Exc.* 2.1-2. See also *Strom.* 4.90.4–91.1 (2.288.7ff.) where Clement claims that the Valentinians transfer the likeness to themselves and teach that the Demiurge was unaware of the superior Spirit being inserted into the man. His remarks are corroborated by the Valentinian doctrine in *Exc.* 53 and in *Exc.* 49.1.

[34] *Exc.* 2.1-2. On the sleep of Adam see Gen. 2.21; on the spiritual seeds being distributed to other people see *Exc.* 55.2f.; on the return of the seeds to the Pleroma

see *Exc.* 64. In *Strom.* 4.90.3 (2.288.1–4) the Valentinians are reported to have said that the visible world is not from the Father and that the soul from an intermediate state is created in the image of the Spirit and depends upon the inbreathing of the superior element. Such teachings are also found in several passages of the *Excerpta:* the visible world was created by the psychic Demiurge, not the Father (*Exc.* 47.1f.); the soul or psychic element stands ontologically between the material and spiritual elements (*Exc.* 51.2–3; 53.5 et al); the soul depends on the superior, spiritual element breathed into it (*Exc.* 2.2); and the soul is an image of the Spirit (*Exc.* 50.2; 54.2).

35 *Exc.* 21.2. At some point the spiritual seed placed in Adam seems to have been divided into a male and a female element, but when, how, or why this happened is not clear. The problem lies in the lack of specific information about the seed in this section of the *Excerpta*. On this problem see the discussion in Sagnard, *La Gnose valentinienne*, pp. 552–6.

36 *Exc.* 55.1–56.2. On the garments of skin see Gen. 3.21; on "the first man of the earth" see 1 Cor. 15.47. See also *Exc.* 67.2–3 where it is suggested that human beings must be born so the spiritual seeds can be placed in their souls at birth. Only in this way can the seeds enter the world, undergo the formation according to knowledge, and be saved.

37 *Exc.* 54.1–3. On "the book of the generation of men" see Gen. 5.1; on the true home in heaven see Phil. 3.20; on calling upon the Father see Gen. 4.26; cf. Col. 3.1f.; Gen. 4.26.

38 *Exc.* 69.1–73.3. On the good shepherd and the hired hand see John 10.11–4; on the creation of the evil spirits, including their ruler the Devil, see *Exc.* 48.2; on the creation of the angels of the Demiurge as rulers of the planetary spheres see Iren. *Adv. Haer.* 1.5.2; on the creation of the Devil and his cohorts as rulers of the world see Iren. *Adv. Haer.* 1.5.4. For a detailed description of the astrological notions underlying this section of the *Excerpta*, see Sagnard, *Extr. de Théod.*, pp. 224f. and the studies cited there.

39 *Exc.* 37–38.3. On the river of fire see Daniel 7.10; on Gehenna see Luke 12.5.

2

The Basilideans and Valentinians
on the Savior and His Church

Basilides and His Followers

ALTHOUGH we have seen how Basilides taught that the souls of human beings are filled with the passions of evil spirits, we also discover in book five of the *Stromateis* how he claimed that certain people are given the gift of faith because they are chosen by God to be saved. Apparently, Basilides thought that faith enables the chosen or elect person to know God, and so faith is not only intellectual in nature, but a distinctive mark of those who are destined to inherit salvation. As an essence, nature, and substance that has been placed in the souls of the elect, faith is so eminently dignified and beautiful that it renders a person worthy of being in the very presence of God. Elsewhere, in the fourth book of the *Stromateis*, Basilides adds to the aforegoing conception when he interprets the words in Genesis: "I am a stranger" on the earth "and a sojourner with you": to mean that the elect are different from the rest of humanity and the world because they are supermundane in nature.[1]

The followers of Basilides expounded a number of ideas like their teacher, for in the second book of the *Stromateis* they say that faith is an innate capacity or quality within the souls of the elect. This faith also allows the elect person to discover things in the divine world through intuition instead of rational argument. Consequently, faith is a divine gift that was given to the elect when they were chosen for salvation in heaven before being born into this world, and therefore, something that is present in the souls of the elect to the degree that they hope to obtain salvation.[2]

In the seventh book of the *Stromateis* the disciples of Basilides are reported to have commented on the transmission of the teachings of Jesus through one of his disciples, Peter. There the Basilideans claim that their teacher was instructed by Glaucias, the interpreter of Peter, and that they possess the doctrines of the apostle Matthias.[3] The first of these assertions simply implies that Basilides stands in a direct line of succession after Glaucias and Peter and thus his teachings are identical with those given by Peter, and ultimately, by Jesus himself. The same apologetic aim underlies the second statement, except that there it is a question of the apostolic authority of Matthias rather than that of Peter. In fact, both of these arguments by the Basilideans were standard polemical devices used by competing Christian groups in the second century to establish the apostolic origin and authenticity of their beliefs and practices.

Further above, in book six of the *Stromateis*, the Basilidean Isidore discusses his opinions on the relationship between the doctrines of the church and those of pagan philosophy in his work entitled *Commentaries on the Prophet Parchor*. In the first book of this commentary Isidore claims:

> the Attics say that some things were revealed to Socrates because a daemon was attendant upon him; and Aristotle says that all men are subject to daemons which follow them during the time of their incarnation, having taken this prophetic teaching and recorded it in his own books without acknowledging the source from which he had stolen it.

Reflecting on the same theme in book two of his work, Isidore also argues:

> and no one should suppose that what we say is a distinctive quality of the elect was said previously by some philosophers; for it is not their discovery; but, having appropriated the idea from the prophets, they attributed it to the one who, according to them, is wise. For it also seems to me that those who lay claim to philosophizing, do so in order that they might learn what the winged oak and the embroidered cloak upon it are—all of which Pherecydes taught concerning God when he spoke allegorically, after taking his argument from the prophecy of Ham.[4]

With these remarks Isidore criticizes the Greeks and particularly, the philosopher Aristotle, for stealing the idea of human beings having a guardian angel from certain prophetic books revered by the Basilideans. Though Isidore only identifies two of these works by name—the *Prophecy of Ham* and the *Prophecy of Parchor*—he is probably referring to Jewish pseudepigrapha that stood outside the canon of scripture or to Christian texts of the same kind. In any case, Isidore believes that these prophetic books are older than the writings of the Greek philosophers and that the latter took the idea of faith as an innate quality of the elect from such books while saying that they had received it from one of their own wise men.[5]

Isidore also does not explain the symbolism of the winged oak and the embroidered cloak, but he asserts that the Greek philosophers seek to learn the meaning of these two figures and that Pherecydes expounded this in an allegory concerning God after he had taken his ideas from the *Prophecy of Ham*. Indeed, it is quite likely that in the allegory of Pherecydes the winged oak was a symbol of the foundation of the earth, which was made by Zeus, and that the embroidered cloak represented Zeus creating the surface of the earth and the ocean surrounding it. If this is so, then discovering the meaning of the winged oak and the embroidered cloak is tantamount to knowing the origin of the world and the identity of its creator. Isidore, therefore, is suggesting that whatever Pherecydes and the other Greek philosophers know about the cosmos and its creator, they have learned from the prophetic books possessed by the Basilideans.[6] By these statements Isidore infers that the teachings of the Basilideans are foreshadowed in Jewish prophecy and the source of the best ideas expressed by the philosophers. Like other Christian apologists in the second century, Isidore tries to demonstrate the greater antiquity and superiority of his own beliefs and practices in comparison to those of his pagan opponents.

Despite the lack of information about the liturgical activities of the Basilideans in Clement's writings, there is a short notice in book one of the *Stromateis* where we are told how some of them celebrated the baptism of Jesus as an annual religious festival. These Basilideans believed that Jesus was baptized on January 6, 29 CE, and so each year on the fifth of that month they conducted an all-night vigil with the reading of scripture. During their vigil, the Basilideans may have read gospel accounts of Jesus' baptism or passages from prophetic texts which were supposed to have predicted that event. These ritual activities also may have been carried out in order to prepare catechumens for baptism on the following day.[7]

Our knowledge of the ethical doctrines of the Basilideans is almost as scanty as that concerning their liturgy. In book three of the *Stromateis*, though, we learn how certain Basilideans formulated some definite ideas about marriage and sex. These Basilideans are quoted as saying:

> when the apostles inquired whether it is better not to marry, the Lord replied with the words: "Not all find room for this statement," "for there are eunuchs", some from birth, others out of necessity.

The Basilideans go on to explain the preceding statement of Jesus by asserting:

> some men have a natural repulsion toward women from birth; those who have this natural temperament do well by not marrying. The latter are the eunuchs from birth. But the ones out of necessity, those are the theatrical ascetics, who subdue themselves on account of the attraction of glory. Therefore, the ones who are eunuchs out of necessity are not so in accordance with reason. But the ones who have made themselves eunuchs for the sake of the eternal kingdom adopt this reasoning because of the things that coincide with marriage, since they fear the hindrance of having to procure the necessities for a family. And in the statement: "It is better to marry than to burn": the apostle means: "Do not cast your soul into the fire by abstaining night

and day, and fearing lest you fall from continence; for a soul that is concerned with abstinence has lost hope."[8]

The Basilideans who are cited above interpret Jesus' statement about eunuchs as a symbolic reference to three kinds of celibate persons: men who should remain celibate because they are naturally adverse to women from the time of their birth; those who are celibate, but without any good reason, because they seek to obtain fame for being continent; and those who have chosen celibacy in order to concentrate on attaining salvation instead of being distracted by having to support a family. Throughout their discussion the Basilideans imply that it is better for a person not to marry, provided that the state of celibacy has been dictated by their natural constitution or chosen voluntarily for the sake of pursuing salvation. On the other hand, the Basilideans do leave room for the different capacities of individual human beings by interpreting Paul's injunction in 1 Corinthians as a recommendation for those who desire sex to go ahead and get married. According to these disciples of Basilides, it is better for a person to marry than to lose confidence in their ability to remain chaste, and thereby, end up falling into sexual immorality.

Immediately after the statements above, Clement quotes a passage from a book written by Isidore, the son and disciple of Basilides. In the book entitled *Ethics*, Isidore states:

> therefore, abstain from a quarrelsome woman so that you might not be dragged from the grace of God, and when you have cast off the fire of the seed, pray conscientiously. But when your prayer of thanksgiving gives way to a prayer of request, and you ask not to trip up in the future rather than to do what is right, then marry. And whoever is young or poor or borne down, and does not wish to marry in accordance with the apostle's statement, let this one not be separated from his brother; let him say: "I have come into the sanctuary; I can suffer nothing." But if he suspects that he might fall, let him say: "Brother, put your hand on me so that I might not sin": and he shall receive help both spiritually and physically. Let him only wish to complete what is good and it shall be built upon. And sometimes we say with our mouth that we do not wish to sin, but our mind is intent on sinning. Such a person does not do what he wishes on account of fear so that punishment may not be meted out to him. And human nature has some things that are necessary and natural and others that are only natural. Therefore, being clothed is necessary and natural, but the sexual pleasures are natural and not necessary.[9]

Like some of his fellow Basilideans, Isidore upholds the ideal of celibacy for those who are capable of being continent and recommends marriage for those who are not. Isidore argues that men should remain celibate if they wish to escape the pitfalls of marriage to a quarrelsome woman or if they are too young, poor, or weak to fulfill the duties of the marital state. In the second place people ought to marry if they are so afraid of committing sin that they pray for help to avoid doing wrong instead of asking for help to do what is right. Those, however, who are continent, should stay within the community of believers so that they can obtain spiritual and physical assistance from their brethren in times of personal weakness. Taking up an idea from Epicurean philosophy, Isidore concludes that the desire for sexual intercourse is natural, but unnecessary, while the desire to be clothed is both natural and necessary. The implication of this last assertion is that the members of the Basilidean community must be content to satisfy only desires which are natural and necessary.

If Clement's account in this part of the *Stromateis* is accurate, as it seems to be, the austere marriage ethic of Isidore and his fellows was discarded by some later members of the Basilidean community.   Apparently, these Basilideans engaged in libertine marital and sexual practices because they believed that they were spiritually perfect and destined for salvation from birth, regardless of their actions in the present. Our lack of detailed information about these people prevents us from knowing exactly why they adopted an ethical stance which differed from that of their predecessors. Perhaps their libertine ethic was formulated as a protest against the asceticism of their fellow Basilideans or as an expression of their own identity as an elite group of people who were not bound by the standards of conventional morality. At all events, their opposition to the ethics of Isidore and his followers was probably an exception, not the rule, among the Basilideans.[10]

As seen in a series of citations made by Clement in the fourth book of the *Stromateis*, Basilides himself adhered to a strict code of ethics, at least with respect to the question of martyrdom. In book twenty-three of his *Exegetica*, Basilides declares:

for I say, therefore, all those who fall under the afflictions mentioned are led to this good end by the kindness of the one who leads them; whether they have forgotten that they have sinned in other matters, they are actually accused of other things so that they might not suffer as those condemned for evil deeds which have been confessed, or be reproached as the adulterer or the murderer, but because they are Christians by nature—the very thing which will console them so they do not seem to be suffering. And even if someone who has not sinned at all happens upon suffering—a rare thing—yet not even this person shall suffer anything in the plot of power against him; but he shall suffer as the child also suffered—the child who seems not to have sinned.

Therefore, as the child (who has not sinned before or who has not actually sinned, but has the sinful element within him) receives a benefit when he is cast under suffering since he gains many hardships: so, indeed, even if a grown man may not have sinned in fact, but suffers, whatever he suffers, this he suffers like the child. For, having the sinful element within himself, he did not sin because he did not have the opportunity to do so. Therefore, we must not impute sinlessness to him. For, as one who wishes to commit adultery is an adulterer even if he does not happen to commit adultery, and the one who wishes to commit murder is a murderer even if he is unable to commit murder, so also if I see the sinless man about whom I speak suffering, I shall say that he is evil for wishing to sin even if the man has done nothing wrong. For I shall say anything rather than call providence evil. Nevertheless, if in passing over all of these statements you wish to put me to shame through certain persons by saying (if it happens): "Therefore, so and so sinned, for so and so suffered": I shall say, if you permit, that he did not sin, but he was like the suffering child. Moreover, if you should press the argument more forcefully, I shall say that whatever man you name is a man, but God is righteous. For as someone said: "No one is free from filth."[11]

Basilides attempts to justify Christian martyrdom in this passage by explaining how the suffering of the martyrs allows them to atone for sins which they have committed in the past but forgotten. According to Basilides, martyrdom is actually a blessing bestowed by God on Christians because the martyrs are able to endure their suffering since they believe that they are being unjustly punished for their faith. In fact, no one who is truly innocent ever suffers, and if a seemingly innocent person, like a child, does suffer, they are being punished for their desire to commit sin even though they have not yet had the opportunity to do something wrong. In response to the remarks of some critics Basilides admits that even if his opponents could point to an innocent person who had suffered, he would insist that that person suffered for their desire to commit sin because no one, except God, is always good.

Just below the passage above, Basilides is accused of thinking that the soul undergoes reincarnation in order to atone for the sins of its previous life. Basilides is also charged with teaching that the soul only suffers punishment in proportion to the sins which it has committed, and therefore, God allows Christians to expiate their sins in the most honorable way through martyrdom. It seems that the soul was supposed to pass through a series of incarnations until it was able to atone for all of its sins and attain a state of perfect purity while still in the body.[12] Subsequently, Basilides says that God does not wish for people to desire or hate anything, but wants them to love everything that exists or occurs in the world because it is part of the whole. Given the fact that this statement appears in the context of Basilides' opinions on martyrdom, the latter may have intended it as an injunction for his followers to accept martyrdom as part of God's plan to let them atone for their sins and be saved. In another passage of the fourth book of the *Stromateis*, Basilides insists that only those sins which are committed involuntarily or in ignorance do not require atonement. Elsewhere, in part of the *Excerpta*, the followers of Basilides interpret a text in Deuteronomy about God repaying the disobedient "to the third and fourth generations" as a reference to the multiple incarnations of a person's soul.[13]

Valentinus

Clement does not give us any other information on the teachings of the Basilideans in his extant writings; but in book three of the *Stromateis* he cites a portion from a letter written by Valentinus to a man named Agathopus. In the brief passage Valentinus says:

> enduring all things, he was continent; Jesus practiced divinity; he ate and drank in his own way and did not evacuate waste. The power of continence for him was such that even the nourishment in him was not subject to decay, since he did not possess corruption.[14]

Here Valentinus sets forth a docetic Christology by explaining how Jesus had a body that was psychic in nature, and therefore, not subject to limitation or corruption as the material bodies of human beings. Without specifically acknowledging it, Valentinus infers that the example of Jesus shows how members of the psychic race can escape from the corruption of the material world by practicing continence and other good works.

In book six of the *Stromateis*, Valentinus also explains in part of his homily "About Friends" how some of the doctrines of the church are identical to those found in the writings of pagan authors. Valentinus suggests that this is due to the fact that pagans have taken doctrines from Jewish and Christian writings and claimed them as their own. He further argues that these doctrines constitute a moral law which God has inscribed on the souls of certain people like words written in a book. Valentinus concludes that people who have this moral law within them are those who really love God and who are loved by God. Thus Valentinus agrees with Isidore that the similarity between the doctrines of Christians and pagans is a result of plagiarism by the latter. Indeed,

Valentinus's remarks here may have been the source of the idea held by his followers, namely, that teachings about God have been preserved throughout history by members of the spiritual race.[15]

Valentinus himself has a few things to say about the spiritual race in a short fragment that is quoted from one of his homilies in book four of the *Stromateis*. In the fragment Valentinus tells the members of his audience that they have been immortal from the beginning and are children of eternal life. He also reminds his listeners that they have asked for death to be distributed among them so they can destroy it. Valentinus ends by assuring his disciples that when they have finally conquered death, they will rule over everything with the unbegotten Father.[16]

The founder of the Valentinian movement takes up the further question of how people are saved from death in another fragment from one of his writings in book two of the *Stromateis*. With a quotation from the Gospel of Matthew, Valentinus states:

> "there is one who is good," whose authority of speech is the manifestation through the Son, and only through him can the heart become pure when every evil spirit is driven from it. For the many spirits which dwell in it do not allow it to be pure; but each of them performs its own works by insulting it variously with desires that are not fitting. And it seems to me that the heart suffers something like an inn; for the latter also is perforated and dug up and is often full of dung since men dwell lasciviously in it and take no forethought for the place, as it belongs to someone else who established it. In the same way the heart also is impure as long as it does not obtain forethought, since it is a habitation of many demons. But when the only good Father shall visit the heart, it is made holy and shines with light; and he who has such a heart is blessed because he shall see God.[17]

Valentinus explains in this passage how evil spirits inhabit the souls of human beings and fill them with unseemly passions. He supports this assertion by claiming that people care as little for their souls, which are ravaged by the passions, as camel drivers care for a caravan station that is full of dung and belongs to someone else. To be sure, the soul can only be cleansed of its passions when it becomes concerned about its condition and is visited by the Son, who is a manifestation of the Father. Valentinus probably thinks that this cleansing occurs when the Holy Spirit enters the soul at baptism and the spiritual element is awakened from its ignorance and enlightened with knowledge of God. In any case, Valentinus affirms that those who possess this kind of soul are blessed because they are destined to contemplate the Father in the Pleroma at the end of time.

The Valentinians

The Valentinians in the *Excerpta* follow the founder of their community by contending that the coming of the Savior was necessary to save human beings from the power of death. The Valentinians say:

> therefore, after the kingdom of death had made a great and specious promise (but nonetheless had become a ministry of death), and every principle and divinity had refused, the great champion Jesus Christ, taking the church upon himself by his own power—the elect and the called: the one, the spiritual element from the one who gave birth; the other, the psychic element from the dispensation—saved and raised up that which he received, and through them also the things consubstantial to them. "For if the first fruits are holy, the dough is also; and if the root is holy, so are the branches."
>
> So he first put on the seed from the one who gave birth, not being contained by it, but containing it with power—this which is formed little by little through knowledge.
>
> And having come into Place, Jesus found the Christ to put on— the one who was proclaimed in advance, whom the prophets and the law announced.
>
> But also this psychic Christ, whom he put on, was invisible; and it was necessary that the one who came into the world be seen here, be held, be a citizen, and hold onto a sensible body. Therefore, a body was created for him from the invisible psychic substance and came into the sensible world by the power of a divine preparation. Thus the words: "The Holy Spirit shall come upon you": mean the origin of the body of the Lord, and: "A power of the Most High shall overshadow you": indicates the formation by God, which he imprinted on the body in the virgin.[18]

The disciples of Valentinus describe in this passage how the Savior came down into the world like a champion athlete to save the spiritual seeds and the souls of human beings. The coming of the Savior was necessary because the material world had become a place of death even though the Demiurge had promised to give life to people if they obeyed the commandments of the Jewish law. In his descent the Savior took the whole church upon himself, including the "elect" spiritual element that Sophia had put forth and the "called" psychic element that the Demiurge had fashioned. First, the Savior clothed himself with the spiritual element by containing it within himself instead of being contained by it. Then the Savior clothed himself with the psychic element by putting on the psychic Christ in the realm of the Demiurge. As the son of the

Demiurge, this Christ was the one whose coming had been predicted by the Jewish prophets; yet he was only an image of the Savior because he was psychic rather than spiritual in nature. By taking the psychic and spiritual elements upon himself the Savior was prepared to save them and the other elements like them that were already in the world.

Since the psychic Christ was invisible, the Savior adapted himself to the conditions of the material world so that he could be seen and touched by human beings. Sophia supplied the invisible substance for the Savior's body from the psychic element that had been created from her passion, and through his skill as a divine craftsman the Demiurge gave this substance form in the womb of the virgin Mary. Consequently, Jesus, who appeared in the world, was not subject to the limitations of physical existence because his visible body was not material in nature. Nevertheless, as the Valentinians say elsewhere in the *Excerpta*, the psychic body of Jesus was inferior to the spiritual nature of the Only-begotten Son.[19]

A different version of the Savior's descent into the material world is given in other parts of the *Excerpta* by Theodotus and some of his followers. They claim that the Savior was a manifestation of the Logos in the Pleroma and that during his descent the Savior put on the spiritual seeds which Sophia had brought forth as a fleshly garment for him. These spiritual seeds were identical in nature with the Savior and Sophia, and they represented the spiritual element in the soul of each person who was to become a member of the Valentinian church.[20]

Interpreting some material in the gospels of Matthew and Luke, the Valentinians in the *Excerpta* also contend that a new star appeared in the heavens when the Savior came into the material world. The Valentinians say:

> on account of this, the Lord came down from heaven to bring peace to those on earth; as the apostle says: "Peace on earth and glory in the heights". It is for this reason that a strange and new star appeared, destroying the ancient astral arrangement, shining with a new, unearthly light, and turning people toward new ways and salvations: as the Lord himself, the guide of men, who came down to earth in order to change from fate to providence those who believed in Christ.
>
> But the results predicted from the position of the stars show that fate exists for the others; and the speculation of astrology is also a clear proof.[21]

The Valentinians explain in these statements how a star in the heavens indicated that the Savior came into the world to save human beings from fate and turn them to a new way of peace and salvation through his providence. By appearing suddenly in the sky the new star upset the ancient arrangement of the heavenly bodies and demonstrated how the Savior was going to destroy the power that fate exercised over humankind. Those people who refused to believe in Christ, however, were doomed to remain enslaved to fate, as shown by the predictions of the astrologers.

The disciples of Valentinus continue their narrative in the *Excerpta* by arguing that the new star in the heavens told the Magi about a king being born among the pious. The king or Savior had come down to the Jews first because they were the only people who were famous for being pious at that time.[22] Further above, in another section of the *Excerpta*, the Valentinians say that the psychic element put on by Jesus grew in faith and good works, just as the spiritual element in him advanced little by little through knowledge until it reached maturity. Without explicitly stating this, the Valentinians suggest that the growth of Jesus in wisdom and stature symbolizes the way in which the soul of a person must grow through faith and good works while their spiritual element or seed must be transformed by acquiring knowledge of the Father.[23]

The Valentinians in the *Excerpta* also give their unique interpretation to other aspects of the life of Jesus which are reported in the New Testament. In one passage the Valentinians explain how Jesus was baptized in order that the male angels might be reunited with their female counterparts, the spiritual seeds. The baptism of Jesus divided the male angels so that they might be baptized, too, and thus be reunited with the spiritual seeds in the Pleroma at the end of time. The reunion of the male angels and spiritual seeds was destined to bring the Pleroma back to its original state of harmony and unity—a state which had been disrupted when the Savior left it to become a comforter for Sophia and descend into the material world.[24]

Theodotus and some other Valentinians complement the aforegoing account by interpreting the descent of the dove at the baptism of Jesus in relationship to their own ideas about redemption. First, the Valentinians say that the dove, which appeared as a body, was the Spirit of the Father's thought and that this is what made its descent upon the flesh of the Logos. Subsequently, Theodotus and his disciples claim:

> ...the redemption of the name...came down upon Jesus in the dove and redeemed him. And Jesus also had need of redemption so that he might not be held back by the thought of the deficiency in which he had been placed, as he came forth through Sophia.[25]

Through these last remarks the Valentinians of the eastern school depict the Spirit of the Savior descending upon Jesus in the form of a dove and giving him the redemption of the name. As a result of his redemption, Jesus was filled with all of the power of the Aeons in the Pleroma and thereby ensured that he would escape from the Devil and the other evil spirits who were seeking to keep him in the material world. Accordingly, the experience of Jesus shows how human beings can escape from the tyranny of the demons and the material world by being baptized and receiving the Holy Spirit.

Near the end of the *Excerpta*, the Valentinians interpret parts of the canonical gospels to portray Jesus being tempted by the evil spirits after his baptism. Quoting a passage from the Gospel of Luke, the Valentinians explain that Jesus was baptized into God, and therefore, acquired the "power to walk superior to scorpions and snakes"—the evil powers. The Valentinians also cite some phrases from the Gospel of Mark to say:

> after his baptism the Lord was shaken, as our example, and was first "with the beasts" "in the desert"; then, when he had conquered these and their ruler, he was ministered to by angels because he was already a true king. For the one who had conquered angels in the flesh was now, with good reason, served by angels.

With their description of Jesus in the passages above the Valentinians assert that every person who is given the Spirit at baptism will overcome the temptations of the Devil and his cohorts in the future. In fact, Jesus' resistance to temptation reveals how the members of the Valentinian community shall also rule over the powers of the material world and be served like kings by their male angels.[26]

At the beginning of the *Excerpta* the Valentinians interpret other accounts in the canonical gospels to argue that those whom Jesus raised from the dead were only an image of the spiritual resurrection. The Valentinians affirm that this is the case because Jesus left the bodies that he raised in a corruptible form so they would eventually die like other bodies of a material nature. By raising the dead Jesus indicated that the material body shall die while the spiritual element shall be resurrected and escape from death and corruption.[27]

The Valentinians comment on Jesus' method of teaching in another section of the *Excerpta* where they claim that he instructed his disciples with allegories and parables in public and with literal statements in private. A little further on the Valentinians report:

> and when the Savior said to Salome: "Death will last as long as women bear": he did not mean to reproach birth, which is necessary for the salvation of those who believe. For this birth must exist until the seed which was chosen beforehand has been put forth. But he was making an allusion to the female above whose passions became creation—the one who also put forth the substances without form, and on whose account the Lord came down to drag us from passion and adopt us as his sons.[28]

The followers of Valentinus illustrate in this last passage how Jesus employed figurative language to tell his disciple Salome that death will continue until all of the seeds which were put forth by Sophia have come into the material world. Far from condemning procreation, the Savior's statement suggests that more people must be brought into the world so the remaining spiritual seeds can be placed in souls. As soon as the soul of a chosen person receives the spiritual element and is born in a material body, the Savior can liberate that person by dragging them away from the passions and adopting them as one of his sons. In this manner the remark given to Salome not only explains why the members of the spiritual race must come into a world of becoming and death, but how symbolic interpretation is necessary to understand some of the teachings of the Savior.

Other statements of Jesus recorded in the gospels of Matthew and John are also interpreted by the Valentinians in the *Excerpta* to show how the Savior taught people about the spiritual and psychic elements within them. The Valentinians say:

> ...the Savior placed the spiritual seed in the soul. On account of this, the Savior said: "Be saved, you and your soul". Therefore, having come, the Savior awakened the soul and kindled the spark (σπινθῆρα), for the words of the Lord are power. For this reason, he said: "Let your light shine before men".

Further below, in a different section of the *Excerpta*, the Valentinians add to their discussion of the Savior's teaching when they state:

> therefore, since we were counted together and manifested in the beginning, the Savior said: "Let your light shine": to indicate the light that appeared and gave form—the light about which the apostle said: "Which enlightens every man who comes into the world": that is, the man of the superior seed. For when man was enlightened, then he came into the world, that is, he put himself in order by separating from himself the passions which were mixed in him and which darkened him.[29]

The Valentinians explain in the aforegoing passages how the Savior exhorted his listeners to save both their psychic and spiritual elements. The Savior awakened people from their ignorance by telling them about the spiritual element in their souls, and he enlightened them by describing how that element constitutes the true self of those who belong to the spiritual race. Through his teaching the Savior also revealed that he was the one who appeared to Sophia and gave her knowledge about herself and the things in the Pleroma.

Consequently, the apostle John identified the Savior as the light which illuminates the soul of every elect person who comes into the world. When such a person obtains knowledge from the teachings of the Savior, they are liberated from the passions and the ignorance that have kept them in thrall.

Combining material from the canonical gospels and Romans, the Valentinians go on in another passage of the *Excerpta* to state that the Savior exhorted people to destroy the material element in their souls. There the Valentinians say:

> about these two, the Savior also said: It is necessary to fear "the one who is able to destroy" this "soul and" this "body", the psychic one, "in Gehenna". The Savior called this fleshly element an "adversary," and Paul called it "a law warring against the law of my mind". And the Savior advised us "to bind" and "seize" it like "the things" of "a strong man" who makes war against the heavenly soul; and he advised us "to settle with him on the way" lest we fall into prison and punishment. And in the same way he advised us "to make friends" with it—not nourishing and strengthening it by the power of our sins, but, henceforth, putting it to death now and manifesting its fading character by abstinence from evil: so that in this separation it might be dispersed and evaporated in secret, and, not having received any substance in itself, it might not have permanent strength in its passage through the fire. This is called a "tare" that grows up with the soul— with the good seed. This is also a seed of the Devil, because it is consubstantial with him, and a snake, a supplanter, and a robber, attacking the head of a king.[30]

The Valentinians here depict the Savior telling people how to resolve the conflict between the material element or passions and the psychic element or soul within them. On the one hand, the Savior warned people to fear the Devil because the latter has the power to fill their souls with passion, and thereby, cause them to commit sin and become subject to punishment and destruction. The Savior also explained to his listeners that if they abstain from sin during their sojourn in the world, they will gradually eliminate the passions from their souls and deprive the Devil of his power over them. The Savior assured people that through the destruction of the passions in their souls they will contribute to the progressive dissolution of the material world—a world which is destined to be consumed by fire at the end of time.

The followers of Valentinus take up a number of other quotations in the *Excerpta* to interpret Jesus' instruction about the payment of taxes as a reference to the human soul. The Valentinians argue:

in the case of the coin brought to him the Lord did not say: "Whose possession?": but: "Whose image and inscription?" The apostles answered: "Caesar's": so that it might be given to the one to whom it belongs. So also through Christ the faithful one has the name of God as an inscription and the Spirit as an image. Even the irrational animals show to whom they belong and are claimed by a seal. And so the faithful soul carries about "the marks of Christ" when it has received the seal of the truth. These are "the children" who now rest "in bed"; these are "the wise" virgins, with whom the others, who were late, did not enter into the good things which have been prepared—things "into which angels desire to gaze."[31]

These remarks by the Valentinians show the Savior teaching his disciples that a soul inscribed with the name of God will be given to the Father, just as a coin stamped with the image of Caesar is given to the emperor. The Savior's response to his disciples infers that the faithful soul obtains the name of God when the Holy Spirit enters it during baptism. Through the indwelling of the Spirit, God is able to recognize and claim the faithful soul as his own, much like people are able to identify their property by its distinctive brand or seal. For the Valentinians, the souls of faithful people are those to whom the Savior referred in his parables about the children resting in bed and the wise virgins who were prepared for the marriage banquet. These are the ones who are destined to receive the same reward of salvation as their male angels.

In a different part of the *Excerpta* the Valentinians describe how the Savior taught people about his identity with the Father and the Aeons, Life and Truth, and in so doing indicated that his true nature was not psychic. Further above, Theodotus contends that the Savior called himself "the Door" to signify the manner in which he was going to gather the spiritual seeds into the eighth heaven and lead them across the Limit and into the Pleroma. Certain other Valentinians also assert that the Savior predicted how the psychic Christ would be raised up next to the Demiurge after the crucifixion of the psychic body of Jesus. The Savior himself further revealed that he would raise up all of the souls containing the spiritual element and bring them into the eighth heaven with himself.[32]

Commenting on selected aspects of the passion narratives in the New Testament, Theodotus and his followers say that the cross is a sign of the Limit because it separates the unfaithful from the faithful in the same way that the Limit separates the world from the Pleroma. Consequently, Jesus bore the cross on his shoulders to symbolize the Savior separating the faithful from the unfaithful and leading the spiritual seeds past the Limit and into the Pleroma. The Jews, who were members of the psychic race, knew the names of Jesus and Christ because the coming of the messiah had been prophesied in their writings;

but they were unaware of the true meaning of Jesus bearing the cross since they did not expect the messiah to suffer. At the beginning of the *Excerpta*, the Valentinians state that while he was on the cross, Jesus deposited the whole spiritual seed (collectively called Sophia) so it might not be detained in the material world by the demons. This seed (σπέρμα) was the spiritual element of the elect (τοὺς ἐκλεκτούς) or members of the Valentinian church. The Savior himself was remitted to the Demiurge at the same time as the spiritual seed, though a material or psychic substance remained on the cross to suffer and die.[33]

Some other Valentinians give a different account of the crucifixion in a subsequent passage of the *Excerpta* when they explain how the psychic Christ deposited himself into the hands of the Demiurge while the visible body of Jesus suffered and died on the cross. Since the spiritual seeds were in the psychic Christ, they also were committed into the hands of the Demiurge. The Savior, however, was withdrawn from the psychic body of Jesus because death cannot conquer anything that is spiritual in nature and nothing psychic can die as long as the Spirit of life is in it. Indeed, the escape of the psychic Christ and the seeds demonstrates how the souls of elect persons will be saved from death and raised above the material world by virtue of the spiritual element within them.[34]

The followers of Valentinus in the *Excerpta* interpret further material from the canonical gospels to argue that prophecy was fulfilled when the visible body of Jesus and not his "bone," the psychic Christ, was pierced on the cross. The flow of water and blood from the side of Jesus also represented the passions being eliminated from the souls of people. Therefore, the Savior raised up the psychic body of Jesus after it had become impassible to illustrate how those who are psychic in nature will be lifted up and saved by him once they are set free of the passions controlling them. Those who are spiritual in nature, though, will be given an even better kind of salvation because they possess their souls as wedding garments enclosing the spiritual seed.[35]

Elsewhere, at the beginning of the *Excerpta*, the Valentinians describe how the Savior removed the material element from his apostles after the resurrection and enlightened their divine "spark" (σπινθῆρα) or spiritual element by giving them the Holy Spirit. The Savior commanded the apostles to preach and to baptize in the threefold name those who believed in him so that such persons might obtain the Holy Spirit, too. Meanwhile, the psychic Christ sat next to the Demiurge to prove to the evil spirits that they had only pierced the psychic body or appearance of Jesus. The Savior also sat down with the Demiurge to prevent the spiritual elements from going into the Pleroma before himself and to keep the Creator from hindering their ascent.[36]

After their time with the Savior following the resurrection, the apostles began to baptize all of those who believed in the Lord. In this way the apostles were able to displace the evil spirits who ruled over the twelve signs of the zodiac and overturn the power of fate that controlled the lives of human beings. Those who received the Spirit from above experienced a spiritual rebirth that guaranteed them eventual liberation from the material world and death. As new members of the church, they possessed the same Spirit that inspired the Jewish prophets and thus were capable of performing miracles of healing and uttering prophecy.[37]

The Valentinians in the *Excerpta* extend their narrative on the history of the early church with a description of the apostle Paul preaching different messages about the Savior to members of the psychic and spiritual races. The Valentinians say:

> Paul became the apostle of the resurrection in the image of the Paraclete. Immediately after the passion of the Lord, he also was sent out to preach. Wherefore he preached the Savior from two points of view: as begotten and passible for the sake of those on the left, because they are able to know him and are afraid of him in this way; and, on the spiritual plane, as coming from the Holy Spirit and the virgin, because the angels on the right know him in this manner.[38]

In a brief remark the Valentinian Theodotus relates how the apostle Paul spoke about being in the flesh as if he were already outside the body and used the word "flesh" in reference to that weakness which was an emanation from the woman above. The Valentinians who are quoted in the seventh book of the *Stromateis* provide a further bit of information by saying that Valentinus was a hearer of Theodas, a disciple of Paul.[39]

From the aforegoing statements, we can see that the Valentinians attempted to trace their distinctive doctrines back to the apostle Paul and thence to the Savior. According to them, Paul preached about Jesus suffering on the cross to members of the psychic race because they were able to identify with the psychic nature of Jesus and therefore were willing to obey his commandments out of fear of punishment. Paul also described on a spiritual plane how the Savior passed through the virgin Mary, for the apostle knew that the male angels and the members of the spiritual race would recognize the Savior in this way as one who was consubstantial with them. Theodotus adds to this portrait of Paul by explaining how the apostle carried on the Savior's teaching concerning the passions of the mother that were cast out of the Pleroma and became the lower Sophia. Other Valentinians argue that their founder stands in the direct line of succession after Theodas and Paul, thereby inferring that their teachings are part of the apostolic doctrine that goes back to the Savior.

Contrary to some people in the ancient world who denied the efficacy of ritual behavior, the Valentinians in the *Excerpta* placed a great value on certain practices, particularly that of baptism. In one specific passage the Valentinians say:

> as the birth of the Savior released us from becoming and fate, so also his baptism set us free from fire and his passion from passion, in order that we might follow him in all things. ...being baptized in the name of the Father and the Son and the Holy Spirit, ...we are reborn and become higher than all the other powers.[40]

The Valentinian teacher Theodotus interprets material from 1 Corinthians to clarify the purpose of baptism in another portion of the *Excerpta*. Theodotus declares:

> and when the apostle said: "Otherwise, what shall they do who are baptized for the dead?" For the angels, of whom we are a part, were baptized for us. And we, who have been mortified by this state of existence, are dead; but the males, who did not partake of this state, are living.[41]

Other Valentinians, who were perhaps the disciples of Theodotus, quote the same passage in 1 Corinthians as above to state:

> "if the dead are not raised, why also are we baptized?" Therefore, we are raised up equal to the angels and restored to the males—the members with the members—in unity.
>
> "Those who are baptized on behalf of the dead" are the angels who are baptized on behalf of us, so that when we also have the name, we may not be held back and be prevented from passing into the Pleroma by the Limit and the cross.
>
> Wherefore, in the imposition of hands, it is said at the end: "For the angelic redemption": that is, for the one which the angels also have, in order that the person who has received the redemption may be baptized in the same name in which his angel was baptized before him.
>
> Now, in the beginning, the angels were baptized in the redemption of the name that came down upon Jesus in the dove and redeemed him.[42]

The Valentinians confirm the importance of ritual in these passages by relating how people are baptized in imitation of the Savior to undergo a spiritual rebirth, become superior in power to the evil spirits, and escape destruction by fire at the end of the world. Theodotus and his followers also interpret the baptism for the dead mentioned in 1 Corinthians as a reference to the male angels of the Savior being baptized on behalf of them. The male angels are called "the living" because they do not exist in the material world while the members of the spiritual race or elect are "the dead" since they have been brought into the world by Sophia. Therefore, the male angels are baptized in the name of Christ and receive the spiritual power of the Pleroma like Jesus so their female counterparts, the elect, can be baptized in the same name and obtain the same spiritual power as them. To facilitate this spiritual transformation, an officiant of the Valentinian community recites the ritual formula: "For the angelic redemption": when he places his hands on the candidate's head during the prebaptismal ceremony. By acquiring the Spirit in imitation of the Savior and his angels the new member of the Valentinian church is assured of being raised up and reunited with his or her male counterpart in the Pleroma.

Even though the Valentinians emphasize the efficacy of baptism in the name of Jesus Christ, they admit that a candidate must engage in fasting, supplication, prayer, and genuflection before being immersed to protect themselves from the vengeful activity of the evil spirits. Such rituals are carried out to prevent the unclean spirits (ἀκάθαρτα πνεύματα) from going down into the water and obtaining the seal of baptism with the candidate. Despite these precautions, the demons attempt to regain control over the person whom they formerly possessed by tempting them with so much power that the newly-baptized person is visibly shaken. The example of Jesus, however, who successfully resisted the temptation of the Devil, guarantees the initiate that he or she will overcome the demons through the power given to them by the Holy Spirit.[43]

The Valentinians in the *Excerpta* provide more details about the way baptism works by explaining how it has both a sensible and an intelligible nature. The Valentinians say:

on the one hand, the corporeal element of the fire takes hold of (ἅπτεται) all bodies; on the other hand, the pure and incorporeal element takes hold of (ἅπτεσθαι) incorporeal things, like demons, evil angels, and the Devil himself. Thus the heavenly fire (πῦρ) is twofold (δισσὸν) in nature—partly intelligible (τὸ μὲν νοητόν) and partly sensible (τὸ δὲ αἰσθητόν).

Therefore, by analogy, baptism is also dual in nature: partly sensible (τὸ μὲν αἰσθητὸν) because it puts out the sensible fire through water; and partly intelligible (τὸ δὲ νοητὸν) because it is a protection against (ἀλεξητήριον) the intelligible fire through the Spirit.

And the corporeal spirit of the sensible fire becomes food and fuel when it is small; but it becomes an extinguisher when it is full. And the Spirit, which is given to us from above, not only masters the elements but also the powers and evil principles because it is incorporeal.[44]

These remarks of the Valentinians show how the fire which flows out from under the throne of the Demiurge is composed of both a sensible and an intelligible part. The sensible part of this fire is destined to dissolve the material bodies of human beings and the visible world as the intelligible part destroys the material powers, that is, the Devil and his cohorts. Accordingly, Christian baptism is purposely designed with a dual aspect to put out the sensible and intelligible parts of the heavenly fire. As the sensible aspect, the water of baptism eliminates the material element or passions from a person's soul. The intelligible aspect or Holy Spirit completes the process by expelling the evil spirits from the soul and protecting the soul from temptation in the future. In fact, the Holy Spirit is capable of overcoming any material object or being because, unlike a small wind that fuels a flame, it is incorporeal and a powerful breath that completely extinguishes the heavenly fire. Elsewhere in the *Excerpta*, the Valentinians describe the Holy Spirit penetrating the bread of the Eucharist and the oil for anointing when the name of God is invoked over these elements during the baptismal ceremony. The Spirit transforms the bread and oil into active spiritual powers by separating the material element from them and sanctifying them so they are pure like the water used for exorcism and baptism.[45]

The Valentinians cite several passages from various texts in the New Testament to contend that baptism is called "death" and "an end of the old life" since the newly-baptized person renounces the evil spirits and is set free from their control. Baptism is also referred to as "life according to Christ" because the initiate acquires the Holy Spirit and thus is empowered to live a pure life in imitation of the Savior. The change wrought by baptism does not affect the person's body, for their physical appearance remains the same as it was before immersion; but it does change the person's soul in so far as the demons are expelled from it and the spiritual element in it is enlightened and given power. In recognition of this transformation the other members of the Valentinian community call the baptized person a "servant of God" and "Lord of the unclean spirits" to signify that such a one is now the property of God and possesses spiritual power that is superior to that of the demons. Henceforth, the predictions of the astrologers regarding the destiny of the baptized person are not valid because the latter is no longer subject to the power of fate. Frustrated by their weakness, the evil spirits tremble in fear before the power of the soul which they once inhabited.[46]

The aforegoing claims are supported by the Valentinians as they contend that those of the spiritual race who have been brought into the world by Sophia are reborn through baptism in Christ and raised up to life in the eighth heaven. Through spiritual rebirth these people die to the world by no longer following the dictates of the passions and by living for God in imitation of the pure life of the Savior. Indeed, those who are spiritually reborn know that they will escape from death and corruption because they have been set free from the demons by the power of the threefold name invoked over them at baptism. They have ceased from bearing the image of the evil spirits and exhibit their true spiritual nature as proof of their identity with the Pleroma.[47]

The Valentinians go on in the *Excerpta* to explain how knowledge plays an integral part in their liberation from the passions and the power of fate. The Valentinians assert:

> it is not only the washing that liberates us, but also the knowledge of who we were, what we have become; where we were, where we have been cast; where we hasten, what we are redeemed from; what is birth, what is rebirth.
>
> So long as the seed is still without form, it is a child of the female; but when it is formed, it is changed into a man and becomes a son of the bridegroom. It is no longer weak and subject to the visible and invisible things of this world; but, having been made a man, it becomes a male fruit.

A little further above, the Valentinians reiterate the same doctrine when they say:

> for as long as we were children of the female alone—being incomplete and childish and foolish and weak and without form, brought forth like abortions, as if from a shameful union—we were children of the woman; but when we have been formed by the Savior, we have become children of a man and a bridechamber.[48]

The terse doctrinal statements in these passages reveal the important role that knowledge played in the Valentinian quest for salvation from the material world and its powers. They infer that knowledge liberates them from ignorance about their divine origin, nature, and destiny in the same way that it set Sophia free when she learned about herself and the Pleroma from the Savior. Those who receive this knowledge through instruction before and after baptism learn that they are identical in essence with the Father, that they were originally one with the Father but became separated from him through the fall of Sophia, and that they are destined to be reunited with the Father at the end of time. By learning about the supreme deity and themselves the members of the spiritual race are divested of the passions that formerly plagued them—passions like the fear of death, anxiety over one's identity, and the desire for material things. Those who obtain such knowledge are not subject to the evil powers because their education has changed them into the likeness of their male angels and made them children of the Savior and the Pleroma rather than offspring of Sophia.

The significance of knowledge in the Valentinian scheme of salvation is corroborated by other testimony from Clement in the second book of the *Stromateis*. There the Valentinians are charged with saying that they are able to acquire knowledge and be saved by nature because of the spiritual element within them, but other Christians are only capable of being faithful due to their psychic nature. Justifying these claims, the Valentinians argue that the knowledge which they possess is as superior to the faith of other Christians as the spiritual nature is to that which is psychic.[49]

Since the Valentinians believed that their salvation was guaranteed by nature, it might be assumed that they placed little value on matters of conduct. The reports given by Clement in the *Stromateis* and *Excerpta*, however, indicate that certain kinds of action were highly regarded by members of the Valentinian community and played a significant role in their soteriology. At the beginning of the third book of the *Stromateis*, Clement remarks that the Valentinians derive the union of wedlock from the divine emanations above and are well-pleased with marriage. In a passage of the *Excerpta*, Theodotus explains how the Savior did not disparage birth when he told Salome that death will last as long as women bear children. The Valentinian teacher adds that birth is necessary for the salvation of those who believe and must continue until the seed which was chosen beforehand is brought forth.[50]

It is possible to see from these reports that the Valentinians mentioned by Clement had a positive attitude toward marriage, sex, and procreation. For them, marriage on earth was an image of the pure and eternal marriages of the Aeons in the Pleroma. Therefore, the Valentinians undoubtedly emphasized spirituality and purity in the conjugal union while disallowing any sexual licence or divorce. By modelling their marriage on that of the Aeons the Valentinian man and woman confirmed their identity with the Pleroma and anticipated their reunion with the male angels at the end of time. Judging from the statements of Theodotus, the Valentinians encouraged sexual intercourse in marriage because only through procreation could the spiritual seeds put forth by Sophia be inserted into the souls of those being born and thus enter the world, undergo the process of redemption, and be saved. Marriage and the procreation of children among the Valentinians was not merely an accommodation to the demands of life in the material world, but a practical means by which the community of the elect could bear fruit like their ancestor Seth and ensure that all of the spiritual seeds would be saved.

The moderate views of the Valentinians regarding marriage are also expressed on the subject of martyrdom by one of their well-known teachers,

Heracleon. In the fourth book of the *Stromateis*, Clement relates how the most esteemed member of the Valentinian school, Heracleon, interprets some of Jesus' statements about confession by saying:

there is a confession by faith and conduct, and one by voice. So the confession by voice that is made in the presence of the authorities is what most people incorrectly consider to be the only confession. But the hypocrites also can make this confession. Yet this saying shall not be found to have been meant generally; for not all those who are saved have made the confession by voice and expired, among whom are Matthew, Philip, Thomas, Levi, and many others. And the confession by voice is also not general, but individual. But what he specifies now is general: the confession by works and actions corresponding to our faith in him. And the individual one, which is made in the presence of the authorities, also follows from this general confession, if it is necessary and reason dictates. For the very one who first confessed rightly with his disposition shall also confess with his voice. And he spoke well by using the expression "in me" in the case of those who confess, and he applied the expression "me" with regard to those who deny. For the latter, even if they confess him with their voice, deny him by not confessing him in their actions. But those alone confess "in him," who live by conduct and actions in accordance with him—those in whom he also confesses, as he holds them and is held by them; wherefore they never can deny him. But those deny him who are not "in him". For he did not say: "Whosoever shall deny "in me": but: "me": since no one who is "in him" shall ever deny him. And the expression "before men" applies to those who are saved and to those who are pagans, and so, by conduct before the former and by voice before the others.[51]

The basic argument of Heracleon in this passage is that there are two kinds of confession: one, when a person lives in imitation of Jesus in accordance with their faith, and another, when a person tells the authorities in a court of law that he or she is a Christian. Heracleon contends that contrary to the opinion of many Christians, those who profess to follow Jesus must confess him with their conduct, though they may not be forced to confess him with their voice before the authorities. The confession by conduct and faith is a universal one because it is incumbent upon all Christians; but the one by voice is individual since it is only necessary in some cases. It is not unusual for a Christian to not have to make a verbal confession before the authorities because a number of Jesus' disciples also did not do this even though they were subsequently reckoned among the saved.

Addressing the problem of hypocrisy, Heracleon cautions his fellow Christians not to think that only the verbal confession is genuine, for even those who deny Jesus with their impure conduct can confess him with their mouth before the authorities. Actually, any one who confesses Jesus with their conduct first will confess him with their voice when brought before the authorities, provided, of course, that a verbal confession is necessary and reasonable in that situation. This kind of person truly lives in imitation of Jesus, just as the Lord lives in them through the indwelling of the Holy Spirit. Heracleon concludes that a person who is completely identified with Jesus in their conduct and faith can no more deny the Lord than the latter can deny himself.

The Valentinians in the *Excerpta* draw their account of things to a close by quoting a variety of scriptural passages to describe the final destiny of humankind. Citing a text in Deuteronomy about God repaying the disobedient "to the third and fourth generations," the Valentinians say that the three places indicate those on the left, the "fourth generation" their own seed, and "showing pity to thousands" those on the right. In another part of the *Excerpta* certain Valentinians quote material from the letters of Paul to claim:

> so the spiritual element is saved by nature; the psychic element, which is free, has a propensity toward faith and incorruption or toward unbelief and corruption, according to its own choice; and the material element is destroyed by nature.
>
> When the psychic element shall be engrafted onto the good olive tree into faith and incorruption and partake "of the fatness of the olive", and when the gentiles shall come in, then "in this way all Israel...". And "Israel" is an allegorical expression for the spiritual man, the one who shall see God, the legitimate son of the faithful Abraham, the one "from the free woman"—not the one "according to the flesh", the one from the Egyptian slave-woman.
>
> Therefore, from the three races there is produced a formation of the spiritual element and a change of the psychic element from slavery to freedom.[52]

The disciples of Valentinus explain in these statements how the material race will be destroyed, the spiritual race saved, and the psychic race saved or lost depending on whether they choose to believe and do good works or not. The members of the spiritual race are in fact the "true Israel," the legitimate descendants of Abraham, and those who shall see the Father because they were brought forth by Sophia after she was freed from her passions. In contrast, the psychic race is the illegitimate descendant of Abraham by virtue of its coming into being when Sophia was still subject to the passions. The end of the world will occur once all those of the spiritual race have obtained knowledge and those of the psychic race who are faithful and good have been changed from a state of slavery to freedom.

Just below, in the same part of the *Excerpta*, the Valentinians say that after their physical bodies die, the souls containing a spiritual element will ascend to the eighth heaven to rest with Sophia while the souls that are faithful, but without a spiritual element, will go up to the seventh heaven to reside with the Demiurge until the end. When all of the souls with the spiritual element have been gathered by the Savior in the eighth heaven, they will be joined by the Demiurge and the souls with him to celebrate their mutual salvation in a marriage feast. Following this feast, the spiritual elements or seeds will leave their souls with the others in the eighth heaven and receive their bridegrooms, the male angels. Then the spiritual seeds and their angels will enter the Pleroma with Sophia and her bridegroom, the Savior, leading the way. In the heavenly realm the spiritual seeds will become Aeons by uniting with their angels in a sacred marriage and engaging thereafter in eternal contemplation of the Father. Through the reintegration of these spiritual beings into the Pleroma the tragic consequences of the fall of Sophia will be reversed and the primordial unity of the divine world will be restored completely.[53]

The Valentinians in the *Excerpta* conclude their eschatology by describing how the Demiurge and the souls remaining with him will stay in the eighth heaven outside the Limit of the Pleroma. As the master of the marriage feast and the best man at the wedding of the spiritual seeds, the Demiurge will rest in complete joy forever by listening to the voice of his friend, the Savior. In this manner the Demiurge will be set free and the psychic elements that are faithful and good will be changed from slavery to freedom once the spiritual elements have been gathered into the Pleroma.[54] The Valentinians end by explaining that the fire pervading the visible world will destroy the evil spirits, people who are material in nature, and the souls of those who have been faithless and wicked. The fire also will destroy the material elements of the world whereupon it will extinguish itself. Thus the Pleroma will be restored to its original unity, the psychic beings who are faithful and good will be saved at a lower level than the spiritual seeds, and the source of evil—the material element—will be eliminated forever.[55]

Notes

¹ *Strom.* 5.3.2 (2.327.19–24); 4.165.3-4 (2.321.27–30). The phrase "but not a power" (ἀλλ οὐκ ἐξουσίαν) in *Strom.* 5.3.2 has been omitted because it does not appear to have been used by Basilides in his interpretation of faith. On "I am a stranger..." see Gen. 23.4 where the words "on the earth" (ἐν τη γη) do not appear. The latter phrase allows Basilides to say that the elect are estranged from the sensible world.

² *Strom.* 2.10.1-2 (2.118.11ff.); 2.10.3-11.1 (2.118.17–21); 2.27.2 (2.127.19ff.).

³ *Strom.* 7.106.4 (3.75.15f.); 108.1 (3.76.22); cf. *Strom.* 3.26.3 (2.208.7ff.). It may be that the Basilideans obtained the doctrine of Matthias from the *Traditions of Matthias* mentioned in *Strom.* 7.82.1–2 (3.58.20–3); on this see Hipp. *Refut.* 7.20.1, as noted in Chadwick, *Alexandrian Christianity,* p. 52 n.70.

⁴ *Strom.* 6.53.2-5 (2.458.19–59.5). On the prophet Parchor mentioned here being identical with the prophet Barcoph named in Eus. *H.E.* 4.7.7 see Foerster, *Gnosis,* vol. 1, p. 74 n.19; on the idea of a guardian daemon see e.g. Plato *Phaedo* 107d–108c; on Pherecydes of Syros, who was a theologian and writer during the sixth century BCE, see Arist. *Metaph.* N4 1091b8 and the excellent discussion in Kirk, Raven, and Schofield, *The Presocratic Philosophers,* 2nd ed., pp. 50–71; on the prophecy of Ham see *Clementine Recognitions* 4.27 where Ham is identified as Zoroaster and credited with being the founder of the art of magic.

⁵ On faith as the distinctive property of the elect see *Strom.* 2.10.1–2 (2.118.11ff.); 2.10.3-11.1 (2.118.17–21); 27.2 (2.127.19ff.); 5.3.2 (2.327.19ff.) discussed above.

⁶ On Zeus making a cloth and decorating it with Earth, Ocean, and the halls of Ocean see Grenfell and Hunt edd., *Greek Papyri,* Ser. II, no. 11, p. 23; on the attribution of the aforementioned fragment to Pherecydes see *Strom.* 6.9.4 (2.429.1f.); on the oak being especially associated with Zeus see the tree at Dodona in *Od.* 14.327f.; on the various interpretations of the oak here see also Kirk, Raven, and Schofield, *The Presocratic Philosophers,* 2nd ed., pp. 63ff.. See also the earth and sea in *Il.* 18.483, which is cited in *Strom.* 6.9.3 (2.428.20f.), and the river Ocean that Hephaestus put on the shield for Achilles in *Il.* 18.607f..

⁷ *Strom.* 1.146.1-3 (2.90.21-4). Note that this is the first explicit Christian testimony to the festival of the Epiphany. The material between *Strom.* 1.146.3-4 (2.90.24-8) has been omitted because it is not at all clear that Clement is attributing these opinions to the Basilideans. In contrast, see the translation in Foerster, *Gnosis,* vol. 1, p. 76.

⁸ *Strom.* 3.1.1-2.2 (2.195.2–96.1). On the reputed statement of Jesus concerning eunuchs see Matt. 19.11f.; on "it is better to marry" see 1 Cor. 7.9; on Paul's views on marriage in general see 1 Cor. 7.1-16, 25-35. The Basilidean version of Jesus' statement in this passage—if Clement's report is complete and accurate—differs considerably from that in the Gospel of Matthew. In the latter case Jesus is credited with mentioning three kinds of eunuchs: those who are eunuchs from birth, those who have been made eunuchs by men, and those who are eunuchs for the sake of the kingdom. The Basilideans, however, cite Jesus mentioning those who are eunuchs from birth and those who are so out of necessity while interpreting his remarks as a reference to three kinds of eunuchs. The deletion of the line in 3.1.3, as suggested in

Chadwick, *Alexandrian Christianity*, p. 40 n.2, and as printed in Foerster, *Gnosis*, vol. 1, p. 79, is retained here. Chadwick points out that the literal interpretation of the word "eunuch" in the sentence under question stands in marked contrast to the figurative interpretation of "eunuch" as a synonym for "celibate" in the rest of the Basilidean passage.

[9] *Strom.* 3.2.2-3.2 (2.196.1–16). The three kinds of desire mentioned here come from Epicurean teaching; see Epicurus *Fr.* 456 Usener.

[10] *Strom.* 3.3.3-4 (2.196.17–21). Whatever the practices of these Basilideans might have been, Clement makes it clear that they were in direct contrast with the emphasis on celibacy, continence, and general restraint in sexual matters advocated by Isidore and the other Basilideans described above. Basilides himself had a strict code of morality as indicated in *Strom.* 4.153.4 (2.316.14f.) where he is reported to have taught that only sins committed involuntarily or in ignorance are forgiven.

[11] *Strom.* 4.81.1-83.2 (2.284.5–85.3). See 1 Peter 4.12-9 upon which Basilides might have based his remarks in this passage; cf. Layton, *The Gnostic Scriptures*, p. 440. See also Plato *Rep.* 2.379b-c, which might have been the source for Basilides' statement about not calling providence evil. On "no one is free from filth" see Job 14.4. The "many hardships" (πολλα... δύσκολα) gained by the child are the sufferings that it experiences. According to Basilides, suffering was a benefit for all human beings who experienced it because through suffering they atoned for the sins which they had committed in a previous life; *Strom.* 4.83.2 (2.285.3–6). Basilides also thought that all sins must be atoned for through suffering, all except those that were done involuntarily or in ignorance; *Strom.* 4.153.4 (2.316.14f.). The "sinful element" (τὸ ἁμαρτῆσαι) in the child refers to the desire, inclination, or potential to commit sin and is synonymous with the "sinful element" (τὸ ἁμαρτητικόν) in the grown man. For Basilides, this desire or potential to commit sin is just as worthy of punishment as a sinful action; cf. Matt. 5.28. The desire, inclination, or potential to commit sin is part of the heterogeneous nature of human beings, according to Basilides in *Strom.* 2.113.2-3 (2.174.17–21); located in the inferior part of the human soul, according to Isidore in *Strom.* 2.114.1-2 (2.174.28ff.); and caused by evil spirits who attach their passions to the rational soul, according to the Basilideans in *Strom.* 2.112.1-113.1 (2.174.6–16). With respect to "so and so," Basilides seems to be referring to Jesus. If that is the case, Basilides is arguing for Jesus' sinfulness and humanity only as a logical outcome of his opponents' premises. Basilides is not saying, however, that he agrees with such premises. Elsewhere, Basilides is described as thinking that Jesus did not suffer; Iren. *Adv. Haer.* 1.24.4.

[12] *Strom.* 4.83.2 (2.285.3–6).). I do not agree with the arguments of P. Nautin against reincarnation as an authentic Basilidean doctrine, as set forth in his article, "Les Fragments de Basilide sur la souffrance et leur interprétation par Clément d' Alexandrie et Origène," *Melanges d' Histoire des Religions*, pp. 393–403. Though Basilides may not be alluding to the doctrine of reincarnation at the beginning of this passage in *Strom.* 4.81.2-3 (2.284.6-12), the fact that he does not expressly state the doctrine here is no proof that he did not teach it. Nautin argues from silence: since the doctrine of reincarnation does not appear in this passage, and it alone would have sufficed to answer the problem of theodicy addressed therein, Basilides must not have espoused the doctrine at all. But the point of this passage in *Strom.* 4.81.2ff. is not to describe the means by which the soul is brought to suffering (reincarnation), but what causes the soul to suffer (sin). The doctrine of reincarnation

is, therefore, neither necessary nor sufficient to answer the question under discussion in *Strom.* 4.81.2ff.. Nautin's arguments against the authenticity of the Basilidean doctrine of reincarnation expressed in *Exc.* 28.1 and that of Basilides in Origen *In Ep. ad Rom.* 5.1 are also to be rejected since they are only based on the hypothesis that Clement's claim in *Strom.* 4.83.2 (2.285.3–6) is false.

[13] *Strom.* 4.86.1 (2.286.3–6); 153.4 (2.316.14f.); *Exc.* 28.1; cf. Deut. 5.9. The progression from the third to the fourth generation and the use of the plural "reincarnations" (ἐνσωματώσεις) in *Exc.* 28.1 implies the possibility of several incarnations for an individual soul.

[14] *Strom.* 3.59.3 (2.223.12–6). Contrary to Foerster, *Gnosis*, vol. 1, p. 239, there is no reason to suppose that Valentinus thought the body of Jesus was spiritual in nature, as some of his disciples in the Oriental school did; Hipp. *Refut.* 6.35.7. Here, as Clement reports in *Strom.* 3.102.3 (2.243.11ff.), Valentinus seems to be portraying Jesus' body as if it were psychic in nature. The members of the Italic school held to the same idea; Hipp. *Refut.* 6.35.6; *Exc.* 59.4–60. The psychic Jesus is the earthly, visible manifestation of Jesus the Savior in the Pleroma. According to Valentinus, only the latter Jesus is spiritual in nature; Iren. *Adv. Haer.* 1.11.1. The earthly Jesus, however, does not possess "corruption" (τὸ φθείρεσθαι) because his psychic body is not material in nature like the bodies of human beings; cf. *Strom.* 3.59.3 (2.223.15f.); *Exc.* 51.1-3; 55.1. He is "continent" (ἐγκρατής) because continence and good works are marks of the psychic element that shall be saved; Iren. *Adv. Haer.* 1.6.2, 4; *Exc.* 56.3.

[15] *Strom.* 6.52.3–53.1 (2.458.11–6); cf. Justin *1 Apol.* 59f.; *Strom.* 1.165.1 (2.103.8f.); 2.20.1 (2.123.7f.) passim. On the idea of Valentinus that the innate quality or capacity is the spiritual seed see *Strom.* 2.36.2-4 (2.132.6-16); on the idea of something being inscribed upon the souls of human beings see *Strom.* 2.114.3–5 (2.174.31–75.9) where the evil spirits are said to dig up and perforate the soul by dwelling in it. The same idea of the soul being imprinted by a spiritual power residing within it is also expressed in *Exc.* 86.2f., except that there it concerns the activity of the Spirit from above; cf. Just. *1 Apol.* 46.2; *2 Apol.* 8.1; 13.2. On the idea of the teaching or knowledge being present in those of the spiritual race see *Exc.* 56.2; on Seth as the ancestor of the spiritual race see *Exc.* 54.1-3.

[16] *Strom.* 4.89.1-4 (2.287.10–5).

[17] *Strom.* 2.114.3-6 (2.174.31–75.14); on "there is one who is good" see Matt. 19.17; on those who shall see God see Matt. 5.8; cf. Plato *Rep.* 579e–80a cited in Layton, *The Gnostic Scriptures*, p. 244.; on the spiritual seed see *Exc.* 3.1-2; on the contemplation of the Father see *Exc.* 64.

[18] *Exc.* 58.1–60.1. The "great and specious promise" (μεγάλην μὲν καὶ εὐπρόσωπον τὴν ἐπαγγελίαν) in this passage refers to the Jewish law, which was given by the Demiurge. The basis for this idea seems to be in Rom. 7.9ff. where Paul says that the commandment (of the law) which promised life proved to be death and in Rom. 5.12ff. where death is said to reign over all men; cf. Sagnard, *Extr. de Théod.*, p. 177 n.1. On the Demiurge as the Jewish Creator who inspired the prophets see *Strom.* 4.90.2 (2.287.27ff.) where Valentinus calls him a "prophet". On "the first fruits" and "the dough" see Rom. 11.16. According to the Valentinians in this passage, the visible body of the Savior was the flesh of the psychic Christ. This body enabled the Jews, who also were psychic, to perceive the messiah that had been foretold in their scripture. Thus the Valentinian Christology here in *Exc.* 58-60

is docetic because it claims that the Savior appeared to have a material body like other human beings when in fact his body was made of a divine psychic substance that would be raised up from the dead; *Exc*. 61.7.

[19] *Exc*. 7.3. The argument in this passage is based on the Valentinian interpretation of "glory as of the Only-begotten" in John 1.14; cf. Iren. *Adv. Haer*. 1.8.5. The Valentinian understanding of the ὡς in John 1.14 as a term of comparison portrays the Jesus who appeared in this world as one who was similar rather than identical to the Only-begotten Son in the Pleroma. Note that Irenaeus attempts to correct the Valentinian interpretation of John 1.14 in *Adv. Haer*. 1.8.5.

[20] *Exc*. 1.1-2; 26.1; 42.3; 17.1. See 1 Cor. 12.12f.; Rom. 12.4f.; Eph. 4.15 for the church as the body of Christ. On the Stoic theory of mixtures behind this passage see Sagnard, *Extr. de Théod*., p. 216.

[21] *Exc*. 74.1-75.1. On the star in the East see Matt. 2.2; on the saying attributed to the multitude of angels see Luke 2.13f.. Note that in *Exc*. 70.1-2 the position of the stars is supposed to indicate the action of the invisible, cosmic powers, though the stars themselves do nothing. By calculating the position of the stars at the time of a person's birth an astrologer is supposed to be able to predict the events that will occur in that individual's life. See the excellent summary of the astrological notions in the *Excerpta* by Sagnard in *Extr. de Théod*., pp. 224–8.

[22] *Exc*. 75.2-3. On the Magi see Matt. 2.1f..

[23] *Exc*. 61.2. Note that in this passage the first part of Luke 2.40: "And the child grew" (τὸ δὲ παιδίον ηὔξανεν): is combined with the first part of Luke 2.52: "And...advanced in wisdom" (καὶ...προέκοπτεν σοφίᾳ). On faith and good works for the psychic element see *Exc*. 56.3; on the spiritual element advancing little by little through knowledge see *Exc*. 59.1.

[24] *Exc*. 36.1-2. On the baptism of Jesus in the canonical gospels see Mark 1.9f.; Matt. 3.13f.; Luke 3.21f.; John 1.29f..

[25] *Exc*. 16; 22.6-7. See the Spirit descending like a dove in Mark 1.10; Matt. 3.16; Luke 3.22; John 1.32. For the Valentinians, the name that descends upon Jesus in the form of a dove is the Spirit or Savior from above. As the common fruit of the Pleroma, the Savior has the name of every Aeon and thus all of the powers of the Father. In *Exc*. 35.2 it is said that the Savior did not need to be redeemed because he already possessed redemption by virtue of being brought forth inside the Pleroma. On the theory of the name taught by the Valentinian Marcus, which is close to the one in this passage of the *Excerpta*, see Sagnard, *Extr. de Théod*., pp. 217ff..

[26] *Exc*. 85.1-2; cf. 76.2. On the "power to walk superior to scorpions and snakes" see Luke 10.19; on the phrases "in the desert" and "with the beasts" see Mark 1.13; on the angels ministering to him see Matt. 4.11 and Mark 1.13; on the evil spirits tempting those who are newly-baptized see *Exc*. 84; on those who are baptized being superior to the evil spirits see *Exc*. 76.4; 80.2-3; on the male angels ministering to those whom they need in order to return to the Pleroma see *Exc*. 35.3-4.

[27] *Exc*. 7.5. On Jesus raising the dead see John 11.44; Matt. 9.24; Mark 5.39; Luke 7.11-7. The spiritual resurrection occurs when the soul is awakened and the spiritual seed is kindled by the Spirit from above during baptism, as shown in *Exc*. 77.2-3; 81.2-3. See also the action performed by the Savior on the apostles after the resurrection in *Exc*. 3.2.

[28] *Exc*. 66; 67.2-4. On Jesus teaching in parables see Matt. 13.10f.; on Jesus

teaching the disciples when they were alone see Mark 4.10; on the Savior's statement in this passage as a reply to a question from Salome see *Strom.* 3.45.3-46.1 (2.217.5–10); on Salome as a disciple of Jesus see NHC II, 2, 43, 25-34; on the importance of the Savior's words see NHC II, 2, 32, 10-4 where those who discover the right interpretation of his sayings are promised immortality. In *Strom.* 3.63.1-2 (2.225.1–6) Clement states that the Savior's words to Salome (like those here in the *Excerpta*) are found in the *Gospel of the Egyptians*. Clement also gives another version of Salome's question and Jesus' reply in *Strom.* 3.64.1-2 (2.225.15–21). Further below, Clement credits Julius Cassianus with citing an exchange between Jesus and Salome that was supposed to have been recorded in the *Gospel of the Egyptians; Strom.* 3.92.2-93.1 (2.238.23–8); cf. *2 Clement* 12.2. In addition, Clement criticizes Cassianus for misinterpreting Jesus' statement and claims that the former departed from the school of Valentinus by teaching encratism in sexual matters like Tatian; *Strom.* 3.92.1 (2.238.18–22). This last contention by Clement implies that the Valentinians did not advocate celibacy—a view which is supported by their interpretation of the Savior's remark in *Exc.* 67.2-4.

[29] *Exc.* 2.2-3.1; 41.2-4. The Savior's statement: "Be saved, you and your soul" (Σώζου σὺ καὶ ἡ ψυχή σου): might be an agraphon or a conflation of Luke 9.24f. and Luke 12.20; on this suggestion see Sagnard, *Extr. de Théod.*, p. 57 n.5. The "you" (σύ) mentioned by the Savior is the spiritual seed or true self of the elect Valentinian, which is enclosed in the soul like a body wrapped in a garment. On the injunction to "let your light shine" see Matt. 5.16; on the light "which enlightens every man" see John 1.9; on the elimination of the passions as a result of the formation through knowledge see *Exc.* 67.4–68; 77.2–3; 79. Note that the Savior recapitulates what he did to the lower Sophia and what Christ did to the Aeons in the Pleroma, as he heals the human soul of its passions and forms the spiritual seed through knowledge; *Exc.* 31.2.

[30] *Exc.* 51.3–53.1. On "the one who is able to destroy" see Matt. 10.28; on Gehenna see *Exc.* 37–38.1; on the "adversary" see Matt. 5.25; Luke 12.58; on the "law warring against my mind" see Rom. 7.23; on the "strong man" see Matt. 12.29; on "settling with him" see Luke 12.58. The word "to settle with" (ἀπηλλάχθαι) in Luke 12.58 literally means "get rid of"; Arndt-Gingrich, *A Greek-English Lexicon of the New Testament*, s.v. ἀπαλλάσσω. The Savior's advice to get rid of and thereby destroy the material soul reveals a basic Valentinian equation: the material world will be dissolved in inverse proportion to the salvation of those of the spiritual race. As Valentinus, quoted in *Strom.* 4.89.3-4 (2.287.14f.), says: ὅταν γὰρ τὸν μὲν κόσμον λύητε, ὑμεῖς δὲ μὴ καταλύησθε κυριεύετε τῆς κτίσεως καὶ τῆς φθορᾶς ἁπάσης. On "to make friends" with him see Matt. 5.25; on the "tare" (ζιζάνιον) and "seed of the Devil" (σπέρμα τοῦ Διαβόλου) that grows with "the good seed" (τῷ χρηστῷ σπέρματι) see Matt. 13.25f., 38f.; on the "snake" (ὄφις) as a "supplanter" or "one who trips up" (διαπτερνιστής = πτερνιστής) see the discussion in Casey, *Exc. ex Theod.*, p. 145; see also Sagnard, *Extr. de Théod.*, p. 169 n.2 on Gen. 3.14f.; 27.36; 49.17; on the "robber" (ληστής) see John 10.1; *Exc.* 72.2.

[31] *Exc.* 86.1-3. On "whose image and inscription" see Mark 12.13-7; Matt. 22.20f.; Luke 20.20-6; on "the marks of Christ" see Gal. 6.17; on "the children in bed" see Luke 11.7; on "the wise" virgins see Matt. 25.1f.; on the good things which have been prepared see 1 Cor. 2.9; on "into which angels desire to gaze" see 1 Pet. 1.12.

[32] *Exc.* 61.1; 26.2-3; 61.4-5. On "I am the life" and "I am the truth" see John 14.6;

11.25; on "I and the Father are one" see John 10.30; on "I am the door" see John 10.7; on the entry of the seeds into the Pleroma with their angels, the Savior, and Sophia see *Exc.* 63.1; 64; 34.2; on Jesus' statements concerning the Son of Man see Mark 8.31; Luke 18.32; 24.7; Matt. 20.18. That which the Savior "put on" (ἀνείληφεν) is the spiritual element, the psychic Christ, and the psychic body, as shown in *Exc.* 58.1–60.1. The Savior, who descended upon Jesus at his baptism, has his own spiritual being apart from these elements. Note also that here the Son of Man is the visible, psychic body of Jesus. This psychic body is filled with and subject to the passions like all psychic elements. In *Exc.* 61.6-7 the passion, death, and resurrection of the psychic body are models of the process by which souls without the spiritual element will be saved.

33 *Exc.* 42.1–43.1; 1.1-2; 26.1. On Christ as the "head" see Eph. 1.22; 4.15; 5.23; Col. 1.18; on various renditions of the saying about taking up one's cross see Luke 14.27; 9.23; Matt. 10.38; 16.24; Mark 8.34. Note that the elect Valentinians, who comprise the spiritual church, will take up their crosses and follow Jesus when they are raised up after death; *Exc.* 63.1.

34 *Exc.* 62.3; 61.6. On "Father, I commit my Spirit" see Luke 23.46. The translation of Casey in *Exc. ex Theod.*, p. 83: "But the spiritual nature referred to as 'bone' is not yet deposited but he keeps it": is incorrect. The spiritual element (τὸ πνευματικὸν) is not referred to "as bone" but is "in the bone" (ἐν τῷ ὀστέῳ). It is the marrow (μυελός) in the bone or soul of Christ; *Exc.* 53.5. Furthermore, Casey mistranslates in saying that this spiritual element is "not yet" deposited. Rather, the spiritual element was "no longer" (οὐκέτι) deposited, for it had to be placed in the hands of the Father or Demiurge before the death of Jesus on the cross; *Exc.* 61.6. The Spirit from above or Savior is withdrawn, just as the spiritual elements are taken away from the psychic body, because nothing spiritual in nature is subject to death. See Sagnard, *Extr. de Théod.*, p. 27 for the suggestion that a psychic substance remained on the cross. See also Kaestli, "Valentinisme Italien et Valentinisme oriental: leurs divergences a propos de la nature du corps de Jesus," pp. 401f. in Layton, ed., *The Rediscovery of Gnosticism*, vol. 1 for the idea that an external, fleshly element remained on the cross. The docetism of the Valentinian Christology is once again seen here in that only the apparent Savior, that is, the visible body which he temporarily inhabited, undergoes suffering and death. The true Savior, the one from above, and the spiritual seeds that are identical in essence with him, do not suffer or die.

35 *Exc.* 62.2; 61.3; 61.6–8. On "a bone of him shall not be broken" see John 19.36; Exodus 12.46; on the "bone" see Genesis 2.23 and the Valentinian interpretation at *Exc.* 51.2; on the piercing of Jesus' side see John 19.34; on the wedding garments see Matt. 22.12. Note that the Savior did not "send forth" the ray of power in *Exc.* 61.7, as in Casey, *Exc. ex Theod.*, p. 81; instead, he "removed" (ἀναστείλας) it.

36 *Exc.* 3.2; 76.3; 62.1–2; 38.3. On the injunction to baptize see Matt. 28.19; on "be seated on my right" see Psalms 109.1; on "whom they pierced" see John 19.37. The episode about the apostles here seems to explain how they received the Spirit without being baptized by the Savior. For others, including Jesus, the Spirit is received only through baptism, as shown by *Exc.* 16; 81.1-3. Note also that the one whom they pierced was the psychic body—the earthly Jesus. Furthermore, the fact that Jesus must subdue Place or the Demiurge in this passage reflects the negative evaluation of the Demiurge in the Oriental school, as shown in *Exc.* 38.2. The Italic school, whose account of the psychic Christ near the Demiurge appears in *Exc.*

62.1–2, attributed evil to the Adversary or Devil and not to the Creator; *Exc.* 52.1f.; Ptolemy *Epistle to Flora* 33.3.5f..

[37] *Exc.* 25.2; 24.1; cf. Joel 2.28f. quoted in Acts 2.17f..

[38] *Exc.* 23.2–3. On the Savior passing through Mary see Iren. *Adv. Haer.* 1.7.2. Here Paul is the image of the Paraclete or Savior because he based his preaching on the fact of the resurrection; cf. 1 Cor. 15.12f.; Rom. 1.3f.. It is precisely the spiritual resurrection that, according to the Valentinians, the Savior came to accomplish; *Exc.* 7.5. This spiritual resurrection is effected when the soul of the elect person is awakened and the spiritual seed or spark of light in their soul is kindled; *Exc.* 3.1-2.

[39] *Exc.* 67.1; cf. Rom. 7.5; *Strom.* 7.106.4-107.1 (3.75.15–8).

[40] *Exc.* 76.1, 3–4.

[41] *Exc.* 22.1-2. On the apostle's question see 1 Cor. 15.29. The Valentinians here are "dead" because they have been placed in a world that is subject to destruction at the end of time; *Exc.* 81.1; 37; 48.4.

[42] *Exc.* 22.3-6; cf. 1 Cor. 15.29. On equal to the angels see Luke 10.36. Note that "they are baptized" (βαπτίζονται) in 1 Cor. 15.29 has been changed to "we are baptized" (βαπτιζόμεθα) in *Exc.* 22.3. The change allows the Valentinians to understand the Pauline passage as a reference to themselves, the dead, being baptized in the same name as their angels in order to be restored to unity. The spiritual seeds are the female counterparts of the male angels because the female and male elements were originally united when Sophia put them forth together in Christ; *Exc.* 39. The male and female elements were taken by Christ into the Pleroma (*Exc.* 23.2; 33.3) where the seeds were purified (*Exc.* 41.2) and existed in the presence of the Savior and his male angels (*Exc.* 41.2; 39). The restoration of the unity of the spiritual seed and their male angels through baptism both anticipates and guarantees their actual reunification in the Pleroma at the end of time; *Exc.* 64. For the Valentinians, redemption did not mean remission of sins as it did for other Christians like Clement; rather, it referred to the reception of the Spirit from above by which evil spirits were expelled from the soul and the spiritual seed in the soul was kindled and given life; *Exc.* 3.2; 77.2-3; 81.2-3.

[43] *Exc.* 83-4; 85.1, 3; cf. John 17.14ff.; Psalms 21.22; Eph. 6.11, 16.

[44] *Exc.* 81.1-3.

[45] *Exc.* 82.1-2. The Eucharist here is not associated with a remembrance of the sacrifice of Christ for the forgiveness of sins, but with a transfer of spiritual power from the bread to the initiate after the bread itself has been transformed. The oil and the water of exorcism (which may have been applied to the forehead of the initiate in the sign of the cross) are magical seals intended to protect the person from the evil spirits by declaring him or her to be the property of the Father. As such, anointing with oil and the water of exorcism was a token of release and protection from the evil spirits. See the discussion of these rituals in Rudolph, *Gnosis*, pp. 228f. and the other texts cited there.

[46] *Exc.* 77.1-78.1. On the idea of baptism as "death" see Rom. 6.3f.; Col. 2.12; on the probable background for calling baptism "an end of the old life" and "life according to Christ" see Rom. 6.4, 11; Col. 2.20; 3.3. Note that in this passage the evil spirits tremble with fear before the power in the newly-baptized one, just as in *Strom.* 2.36.2-4 (2.132.6–16) the angels of the Demiurge are afraid of the power in Adam.

[47] *Exc.* 80.1-3. On Sophia bringing forth the spiritual seeds see *Exc.* 67.4; 68; 79; on the idea of dying to the world and living for God see Rom. 6.10f.; on the demons, evil angels, and Devil as the triad of material beings see *Exc.* 81.1. In Romans, Paul actually speaks of dying to sin while the Valentinian passage here emphasizes dying to the material world. According to the Valentinians, when the material body dies, the spiritual seed enclosed in the soul eludes death and corruption by rising up to the Ogdoad in the same manner that the spiritual element in the soul of Christ escaped death and corruption during the crucifixion of Jesus; *Exc.* 62.3.

[48] *Exc.* 78.2-79; 68. On the change of the female elements into males see also *Exc.* 21.3. The knowledge mentioned in this passage was probably imparted to candidates through catechetical instruction before baptism, recited by them in the credal confession during the baptismal ceremony, and given even more fully to them after baptism as part of their continuing education in the Valentinian community. The formation of the elect Valentinian is a reflection of the "formation according to knowledge" given to Sophia by the Savior; *Exc.* 45.1; Iren. *Adv. Haer.* 1.4.5. Note that in *Exc.* 59.1 and 61.2 the spiritual element within the individual is formed little by little through knowledge until it reaches maturity or perfection. This process of formation or education begins when the individual becomes aware of the spiritual element in his or her soul through the preaching of the Valentinian community; cf. *Exc.* 3.1. It continues after baptism as the elect person receives further instruction in the esoteric doctrines of the group.

[49] *Strom.* 2.10.2-3 (2.118.13-7). On the Valentinian doctrine of salvation by nature see *Exc.* 56.3. See also *Strom.* 4.93.1 (2.289.12f.) where Clement says that the Valentinians, among others, use the word "psychic" as a term of reproach for Christians like himself.

[50] *Strom.* 3.1.1 (2.195.1-2); *Exc.* 67.2-3. On the criticism of the moral standards of the Valentinians see Iren. *Adv. Haer.* 1.13.3-6 against Marcus and his followers and *Adv. Haer.* 1.6.2-4 against certain unspecified Valentinians who supposedly considered conduct on the part of the elect a matter of indifference. On the marriage of the Aeons in the Pleroma or Bridal Chamber see *Exc.* 32.1; 64. The idea that the earthly marriages of the elect reflect the heavenly marriages of the Aeons is an extension of a general Valentinian doctrine taken from Platonism, namely, that the things of the sensible world are a copy of the archetypal things in the intelligible world above. See also *Exc.* 54.3 where Seth is said to bear offspring as spiritual things do. Though it is uncertain whether the Valentinians understood *Exc.* 54.3 in this way, what better method could there be of insuring an increase in the number of the spiritual seed than for the elect to have children? In time, of course, some of these children would grow up, be baptized, and become full-fledged members of the community of the elect.

[51] *Strom.* 4.70.1-72.4 (2.279.27-281.2). On Jesus' statement concerning those who confess or deny him see Luke 12.8f.; Mark 8.38; and Matt. 10.32; on the phrase "in me" see Luke 12.8; Matt. 10.32; on the word "me" see Luke 12.9; Mark 8.38; on the phrase "before men" see Luke 12.8; Matt. 10.32. In contrast to E. Pagels, I do not think that in this passage Heracleon even implies the Valentinians are "exempt from making the second, verbal confession"; see Pagels, "Gnostic and Orthodox Views of Christ's Passion: Paradigms for the Christian Response to Persecution?" in Layton, ed., *The Rediscovery of Gnosticism*, vol. 1, pp. 275ff.. Actually, Heracleon argues that those who confess first by their conduct will also confess with their voice, if they must. Since Heracleon does not exclude himself and his fellow

Valentinians from the Christians who must confess first by their conduct, it stands to reason that he also does not exclude himself and his fellows from those who would confess with their voice if the situation demanded it.

[52] *Exc.* 28.1; 56.3-57. On "to the third and fourth generation" see Deut. 5.9; on "showing pity to thousands" see Deut. 5.10; on the "fatness of the olive" see Rom. 11.17; on "all Israel" being saved see Rom. 11.26; on "the free woman" see Gal. 4.22f.; on "according to the flesh" see Gal. 4.23. See also the interpretation of "Israel" as "the one who shall see God" in Philo *De Abrah.* 52 passim; cf. *Strom.* 1.31.4–5 (2.20.14ff.); 2.20.2 (2.123.10ff.).

[53] *Exc.* 63.1-64. On the parable of the marriage feast see Matt. 22.1-14. See also *Exc.* 35.3-4 where it is said that the angels and the mother are not permitted to enter the Pleroma without the spiritual seeds, and *Exc.* 26.3 and 42.2 where the seeds are brought together and go into the Pleroma with Jesus. Note that in *Exc.* 36.2 the union of the spiritual seeds with their male angels in the Pleroma enables the many to become one and be mixed in the one that was divided on account of them. In this way the female elements that have been changed into men are united with their angels; *Exc.* 21.3. The ascent of the spiritual and psychic elements through the heavens to their final place of repose in the Valentinian schema draws upon eschatological ideas that were part of the general worldview in late antiquity. The idea of the ascent of the soul or spirit into the supermundane realm is a reversal of earlier Egyptian and Greek ideas about the descent of the soul into the underworld.

[54] *Exc.* 34.2; 65.1-2; 49.1; 57; cf. John 3.29. Apparently, the other faithful souls and the psychic Christ, who remain in the Ogdoad with the Demiurge, also partake of the fullness of joy and rest with their creator.

[55] *Exc.* 81.1; 56.3; 48.4. On the fire see *Exc.* 38.1-2; cf. Iren. *Adv. Haer.* 1.7.1; 1.5.4. The fire consumes not only everything that is material in nature on the left, but also the psychic elements or souls of those who have chosen unbelief and corruption; *Exc.* 37.1; 56.3; Iren. *Adv. Haer.* 1.6.1.

3

Clement on the Nature of God, the Savior, and Creation

The Polemic against Basilides and His Followers

NEAR the end of the fourth book of the *Stromateis*, Clement conducts a polemic against the opinions of Basilides on the nature of Righteousness and her daughter Peace. In the midst of discussing the virtues exhibited by Christians, Clement asserts that righteousness is peace of life and a good disposition, to which the Lord dismissed the woman when he said: "Depart in peace." Clement also argues that in the book of Genesis the word "Salem" means "peace" and that Melchizedek—the king and high priest of Salem—was a foreshadowing or type of the Savior. Taking up some ideas that appear in the Epistle to the Hebrews, Clement explains that the name "Melchizedek" means "righteous king" and is in fact a synonym for righteousness and peace, even though Basilides supposes that these last terms are names of divine entities living in the eighth heaven. Thus Clement cites a number of texts in order to prove that the words "righteousness" and "peace" in the scripture actually refer to some of the ethical qualities possessed by people who serve God, and not to certain divine beings, as Basilides claims.[1]

In the second book of the *Stromateis*, Clement also draws some material from the book of Psalms and the Greek philosophers to criticize the followers of Basilides for their description of the terror of the Ruler. Following his discussion of this Basilidean teaching, Clement declares:

> but since the first principle is one, as shall be shown later, these men shall appear to be inventors of twitterings and warblings. And since it seemed useful to God to give a preliminary education from the law and the prophets through the Lord, "the fear of the Lord" is called "the beginning of wisdom"—that which was given by the Lord through Moses for those who are disobedient and hard of heart; for those whom reason does not persuade, fear shall tame them. And foreseeing this from the beginning, the Logos, who educates by each of the methods, adapted an instrument to purify them properly for piety. On the one hand, terror is fear of an unaccustomed appearance or at an unexpected appearance, like a message; on the other hand, fear is an excessive astonishment at either that which comes into being or that which exists. Therefore, they do not see that through terror they have made the god whom they praise as the greatest, a being subject to passion

and in the midst of ignorance before terror. Indeed, if ignorance preceded terror, and terror and fear were "the beginning of the wisdom" of God, it is likely that ignorance causally preceded not only the wisdom of God and the entire creation, but also the restoration of the election itself. Then was it ignorance of good things or of bad things? But if it was of good things, why did it stop with terror? And the ministry and preaching and baptism are superfluous for them. But if it was of bad things, how did evil become the cause of the best things? For if ignorance did not exist beforehand, the minister would not have come down nor would terror have seized the Ruler, as they say, nor would he have received a "beginning of wisdom" from fear for the distinction of both the elect and the things of the world.[2]

Clement attempts to show in the passage above how the disciples of Basilides are wrong for attributing ignorance and terror to the ruler of the world. After announcing his intention to demonstrate at a later time that there is only one supreme deity, Clement refutes the Basilideans by claiming that the fear of the Lord is actually called the beginning of wisdom in the book of Psalms because the Jewish law was given through the Logos and Moses in order to make people fear God and thereby attain wisdom. The Logos or Christ knew that reason alone would not be enough to persuade some people to obey the divine commandments, and therefore, he prescribed certain penalties in the Jewish law to instill fear in those who commit sin and convince such people to live in a pure and pious manner.

Taking a somewhat different approach against his opponents, Clement goes on to argue that the Basilideans have contradicted themselves by praising the Ruler as "the greatest" god while at the same time describing him as being ignorant and passionate before he heard the good news. Clement contends that the Ruler could not have been ignorant of anything good, for this would mean that a good thing—the knowledge of God—was the cause of something evil—the terror of the Ruler. In the same way the Ruler could not have been ignorant of anything evil because then something that is manifestly bad—his ignorance—would have been the cause of such good things as the wisdom of God, the creation of the world, and the salvation of humankind. Consequently, the ruler of the world has never been ignorant of anything, and the Basilideans are completely unjustified in saying that he was enlightened by the Holy Spirit, seized by terror, and given divine wisdom so those who have been chosen for salvation might be separated from the world. Clement concludes that the ministry of Jesus, the preaching of the gospel, and the baptism of believers are actually superfluous in the Basilidean scheme of things because, according to the latter, the ruler of the world was redeemed a long time before the coming of the Savior and the church.

The Polemic against Valentinus

Clement follows up his refutation of the Basilidean doctrine of the Ruler by pointing out the errors implicit in the teachings of Valentinus regarding the fear of the angels who made the first human being. After citing the opinions of Valentinus, Clement states:

> and if fear of the pre-existent Man made the angels plot against their own molded image because the invisible seed of the essence from above was established in the creature, or they were provoked to jealousy by vain opinion (which is unlikely), then the angels became murderers of the creature which had been entrusted to them like a child, and are convicted of the greatest ignorance. Or let us suppose that the angels were moved because they were constrained by foreknowledge. But they would not have plotted against what they foreknew (through which they attempted the deed), nor would they have been struck with terror at their own work, since they would have apprehended the seed from above as a result of foreknowledge. Or suppose, finally, that they undertook the plot because they trusted in their knowledge. This also is impossible, that after learning about the superior thing that was in the Pleroma, they plotted against the Man, and furthermore, seized the thing "according to the image"—the thing which had the archetype in it, and which, with the remaining knowledge, was incorruptible.[3]

Through these brief remarks Clement condemns Valentinus for depicting the angels of the Creator as ignorant and malevolent beings bent on destroying the first man. Clement argues that the angels described by his opponent are guilty of the grossest ignorance if they actually tried to destroy their own creature because they were envious of the man's ability to speak or were afraid of the spiritual power in the Pleroma. First, the angels must have been ignorant of the existence of the spiritual seed before Adam began speaking or else they would not have been surprised by the man's speech and would not have waited until the seed made its presence known before conspiring against it. Secondly, the angels could not have become knowledgeable about the Man in the Pleroma after Adam began to speak, for then they would not have placed themselves in opposition to a being whose power was so much greater than their own. In the last place the angels had to have been completely unaware of the nature of the spiritual element since they did not know that Adam could not be destroyed once he had received the spiritual seed and the knowledge attendant upon it. Without stating this directly, Clement repudiates Valentinus's doctrine because it contradicts his own belief that the angels of the Creator exercised intelligent and benevolent care on behalf of the first human being.

Clement resumes his polemic against Valentinus in a later portion of book two of the *Stromateis* where he criticizes his opponent for thinking that certain people are identical to the supreme deity in nature, essence, or substance. Using some material from various sources in the New Testament, Clement says:

> ...God has no natural relation to us, as the founders of the heresies wish, (whether he made us from nothing or he created us from matter, since the former does not exist at all and the latter is completely different from God), unless someone shall dare to say that we are a part of God and of the same substance as him. And I do not know how anyone who knows God shall suffer to hear the latter when he looks at our life and sees that we are involved in so much evil. For if, indeed, the parts are parts of the whole and form an essential portion of the whole, then it would be—which is not right to say—that God sins in part. But if they are not an essential portion, they also cannot be parts. Yet, since God "is rich in mercy" by nature, he cares for us on account of his goodness, even though we are neither parts of him nor his children by nature. And, truly, the greatest proof of the goodness of God is this: that such being our relationship to him, and being utterly estranged by nature, he still cares for us. For the affection in animals toward their young is natural, and the friendship in like-minded people is the result of intimacy; but the mercy of God is rich toward us who are not related to him in anything—I say, either in our essence, or nature, or the power belonging to our essence, but only in our being the work of his will....[4]

With these statements Clement illustrates how Valentinus and the founders of other "heretical" groups are mistaken in their belief that they and their fellows have the same essence or nature as God. Clement contends that human beings cannot be related to God because their nature is composed of something entirely different from the divine, regardless of whether they are made from nothing or from matter. Likewise, no one who really knows God can honestly say that they are an essential part of the deity when they see how human beings do so many things that are evil. If certain people are essential elements of the deity, then God himself is guilty of committing a sin whenever someone who is a part of him does something wrong. In fact, the greatest proof of God's love for humankind is that he continues to care for people even though they are completely different from him. The mercy exhibited by God toward human beings is so great that it surpasses all other kinds of love, including the affection felt by an animal for its young or that which is expressed between intimate friends. Clement concludes that people are not related to God in nature, essence, or power, but only in the sense that they have been created by an act of his will.

Clement continues his polemic against Valentinus in the fourth book of the *Stromateis* by explaining how his opponent's teaching on the destruction of death by the spiritual race reverses the proper relationship between human beings, Christ, and God. Clement argues that his opponent's hypothesis is incorrect because it makes a select group of human beings rather than Christ the savior of the world, or, at the very least, infers that the members of this group have the same nature as Christ and so share equally with him in the work of salvation.[5] Likewise, Valentinus cannot say that Christ destroys death in order to save the members of the spiritual race, for then he would have to admit that such people do not abolish death by themselves even though they are divine in nature.[6] Furthermore, even if the members of the spiritual race say that they work together with Christ to abolish death, they are still placing themselves and Christ above the Creator of the world by suggesting that they have the power to save what he cannot, namely, the human race. Indeed, if the last supposition were true, Christ himself would be superior to the Creator, and this, in spite of the fact that a son can never be greater than his father, especially among divine beings. Clement abruptly ends his remarks with a promise to finish his argument at a more appropriate time when he will show the heretics once and for all that the Creator of the world and the Father of Jesus Christ are one and the same being. In sum, Clement rejects Valentinus's doctrine about the spiritual race because it elevates certain people to a divine status, and thereby, diminishes the power of God as the Creator of the world and Christ as the Savior of humankind.[7]

The teachings of Valentinus are the object of yet another polemic by Clement in the sixth book of the *Stromateis*. There Clement endeavors to discredit Valentinus by reinterpreting one of his opponent's ideas about the special nature of the body of Jesus. Reflecting on specific aspects of the daily life of Jesus, Clement says:

> but in the case of the Savior it would be ridiculous to suppose that the body, as a body, demanded the ordinary bodily necessities for its duration; for he did not eat for the sake of his body (which was sustained by a holy power), but so that he would not influence those who were with him to think differently about him: just as, of course, later, some did suppose that he was made manifest in appearance; but he was absolutely impassible in that no impression connected with the passions—either pleasure or pain—ever penetrated him.[8]

Here Clement tacitly borrows Valentinus's idea that the body of the Savior was different from that of human beings because it did not need food or drink for its sustenance. Clement, however, reinterprets this idea to assert that the special body of the Savior was still made of flesh even though it was sustained by a holy power and so did not actually need nutrition. Clement further argues that the only reason why the Savior ate and drank at all was to prevent his disciples from thinking that he did not have a real physical body—an erroneous opinion that was later upheld by people like the Valentinians! Hence Clement redefines the teaching of Valentinus to refute the docetic Christology of the latter and his followers. It should be noted, though, that Clement himself comes close to espousing docetism when he states that the Savior was completely impassible; for, in effect, such a statement means that the Savior's body was not fully human because it was not capable of feeling pleasure or pain.

The Polemic against the Valentinians

Although Clement does not comment on the theology of Valentinus anywhere else in his extant writings, he does criticize the disciples of the former for their depiction of the supreme deity. In the same passage of the *Excerpta* where he discusses their opinions about the Depth or unbegotten Father, Clement accuses the Valentinians of forgetting the glory of God by saying that the supreme deity showed sympathy to his female partner, Silence. Since sympathy is actually a passion suffered by one being on behalf of the passion experienced by another, the Valentinians have erroneously attributed passion to the supreme deity through their description of the Depth revealing himself to his companion. They also have made the mistake of ascribing passion to the entire heavenly realm and the spiritual race in their narrative about Christ undergoing a passionate desire to save his mother outside the Pleroma. Clement's point in this passage is simply that the Valentinians have misunderstood the true nature of the divine by assuming that both God and Christ are capable of feeling passions like sympathy and desire—passions which are really antithetical to the very nature of deity.[9]

The Valentinian theology comes under attack in another section of the *Excerpta* as Clement gives a detailed description of his own doctrine concerning the nature of the Son. Quoting material from the Gospel of John and Colossians, Clement explains how he and his fellow Christians say:

> the Logos in its identity is God in God, and therefore, is "in the bosom of the Father"—inseparable, indivisible, and one God....
> And the Only-begotten in its identity—in accordance with whose continuous power the Savior acts—is the light of the church that was

previously in darkness and ignorance.

"And the darkness did not overcome" him: the apostates and the rest of men did not know him, and death did not detain him.[10]

The argument in the passage above is completed in a subsequent part of the *Excerpta* where Clement cites a variety of texts from the scripture to assert:

and "the Logos became flesh" not only when he became a man at his advent, but also "in the beginning" when the Logos in its identity became a son by circumscription and not in essence.

And again, "he became flesh" when he acted through the prophets.

But the Savior is called a child of the Logos in its identity. On account of this, "in the beginning was the Logos, and the Logos was with God"; "what came into being in him is life"; and life is the Lord.

And Paul says: "Put on the new man, the one created according to God": as if stating: "Believe in the one created according to God by God"—the one who is the Logos in God. But the expression: "Created according to God": can mean the end toward which man must reach, in the same way as the statement: "Seize the end for which you were created."

And again, in other passages Paul clearly and explicitly says: "He who is an image of the invisible God". Then he adds: "First-born of all creation". For, on the one hand, he calls the son of the Logos in its identity "an image of the invisible God" and the "First-born of all creation" because he became the creator and originator of all creation and substance when he was begotten without passion; for the Father made all things "by him".

Whence it is also said that he "took the form of a slave", not only his flesh at the advent, but also his substance from that which is subject; and substance is a slave, as it is passive and subject to the active and ruling cause.

For in this way we understand the verse: "I have begotten you before the morning star": as a reference to the Logos of God, the First-created. And in the same way the words: And your "name" is "before the sun" and moon and before all creation.[11]

Clement explains in the passages above how the Logos, Only-begotten, and Savior are names for the same being in order to counter the Valentinian teaching about the emanation of the Ogdoad.[12] Clement affirms that in the first stage of its existence the Logos is the mind of the Father, and therefore, identical in essence or substance with the supreme deity. In the second stage of existence the Logos comes forth from the Father as the Only-begotten Son. As such, the Son is called "a child" of the Logos in its identity because he exists beside the Father as an individual divine being, yet remains one with the Father in essence or substance. The Only-begotten Son is not only identical with the Logos, but also with the Savior who came down to earth. This identity enabled the Savior on earth to act in complete agreement with the will of the Father, enlighten the souls of believers who were formerly in a state of ignorance, and escape from the evil machinations of unbelievers as well as the power of death. Consequently, when the author of the Gospel of John speaks about the Logos becoming flesh, he is referring to it being eternally generated from the Father as the Only-begotten Son, inspiring the Jewish prophets under the old dispensation, and descending into the world as Jesus Christ.

The author of Ephesians makes further references to the Logos by speaking about putting on the new man created according to God to exhort people to believe in Christ. Other passages in Colossians use phrases like "First-born of all creation" and the "image of the invisible God" to show how the Son is the first of all beings to come forth in creation, the one who is begotten without passion, and the instrument by which God created the world. The Son is said to have taken the form of a slave because he became flesh and descended into the world while remaining subject to the will of the Father. For this reason, the book of Psalms mentions the Logos as the one whom God brought forth before making the sun, the moon, and the rest of creation. Thus Clement demonstrates how the Logos, Son, Savior, and Christ are aspects of one being, and not separate entities in the Pleroma, as taught by the Valentinians.

Clement reiterates some of the same points as those above in a different portion of the *Excerpta* when he criticizes the Valentinians for their description of the Christ being put forth outside the Pleroma by Sophia. Immediately after his citation of the Valentinian narrative about Christ entering the heavenly world, Clement quotes material from several passages in the New Testament to argue that his opponents have misunderstood the true nature of the Savior. In contrast to the Valentinians, Clement claims that the Savior is called the "First-born" because he is the first to come forth in creation and is completely subject to the will of the Father. Unlike the Valentinians, Clement also believes that the Savior, Jesus Christ, is the "root" and "head" of every Christian and that the whole church comprises the fruit of the Lord's ministry.[13]

Having opposed the teachings of the Valentinians regarding the nature of the Son, Clement goes on in the *Excerpta* to contradict their opinions about the heavenly world as a whole. Following the Valentinian description of the emanation of the Aeons, Clement quotes a passage from the Gospel of John to say that "all things were made by him" in accordance with the direct activity of the Logos in its identity, that is, all things spiritual, intelligible, and sensible. A little further on in the *Excerpta*, Clement continues to discuss the creation of the heavenly realm by stating:

and the first-created, even if they are several in number, each one is limited and circumscribed; yet the likeness of the creatures exhibits their unity and equality and likeness. Among the seven, there has not been given more to one and less to another; nor is there any advance left for them, since they received perfection from the beginning, at the first creation by God through the Son.[14]

Clement augments the aforegoing account in a subsequent part of the *Excerpta* when he quotes material from several places in the New Testament to claim:

each one of the spiritual beings has its own power and its own ministry; in so far as the first-created were created and received perfection together, their service is common and undivided.

Therefore, the first-created see the Son and themselves and the inferior beings, just as the archangels see the first-created. But the Son is the beginning of the vision of the Father, being called "the face of the Father".

And the angels are intellectual fire and intellectual spirits, who have been purified in their substance.

But the greatest advance from intellectual fire that is completely purified is intellectual light, "into which angels desire to gaze," as Peter says.

But the Son is still more pure than this, being "unapproachable light" and a "power of God"....[15]

The statements in the passages above are set forth by Clement to establish what he considers to be the true account of the creation of the heavenly realm in opposition to that of the Valentinians. Clement explains how the Son has created everything in the heavenly and earthly realms in agreement with the will of the Logos in its identity or mind of the Father. Since the Son is by nature the most pure form of light, he began his creative activity by first making seven angels from intellectual light, and then archangels and angels from intellectual fire. Accordingly, the heavenly world is arranged in a hierarchy that descends from the inapproachable light of the Son to the intellectual light of the first-created angels and thence to the intellectual fire of the lower divine beings. In particular, the seven first-created angels are completely unified and equal in their rank, action, and service to God even though each one of them has its own power and ministry. Moreover, none of the first-created angels can assume a position of superiority over any one of its fellows because they all received perfection when they were created together at the beginning of the intelligible or heavenly realm.

Due to the organization of the heavenly world, the different angels are able to see the other beings on their own level, those on the level just above, and all those in the ranks below. Therefore, the first-created angels are the only ones who can see the Son, that is, the face or beginning of the vision of the Father. Through continuous contemplation of the Son the first-created angels receive knowledge of the supreme deity—knowledge which they pass on to the archangels, who, in turn, transmit it to the lower angels. By doing this the members of each rank in the heavenly realm act as high priests in relationship to those in the rank below them. Each angelic being, however, only receives the knowledge of the Father that it is capable of comprehending, and so a part of the supreme deity remains unknown to all, except the Son.[16] In this manner Clement, unlike the Valentinians, infers that unity and knowledge have always existed in the heavenly world, and thereby, rejects any notion of a divine being disrupting that realm through passion and ignorance.

Commenting on the creation of the intelligible world in book six of the *Stromateis*, Clement attacks the Valentinians and others for supposing that the Creator of the world is lazy because he rested on the seventh day. Clement quotes some material from the writings of Aristobolus and Philo to say:

> therefore, with respect to the rest of God, it is not, "as some suppose," that "God" stopped "doing"; for, since he is good, if he should ever stop doing good, he also would stop being God—which is not right to say. The resting, then, is the ordering, so that "the arrangement" of the things which were made should be preserved inviolate "for all time" and each of the creatures cease from the ancient disorder....[17]

Clement explains in these remarks that the Valentinians and others have misinterpreted the statement in Genesis about God resting on the seventh day as an indication that the Creator of the world is fond of being lazy. In opposition to such views Clement argues that God never ceases to do what is good because it is in his very nature to do good and not otherwise. Consequently, when the book of Genesis mentions God resting after the creation of the intelligible world, it is referring to the Creator arranging the things which he had made so they might remain in proper order and not return to their original state of formless matter or chaos.

Further above, in another part of book six of the *Stromateis*, Clement responds to the Valentinians and other "heretics" who claimed that sin is caused by the fact that human beings are made imperfectly by an imperfect creator. In answer to his opponents Clement states:

> ...we are made by nature, not indeed, so as to have it from the hour of birth, but to be fit for acquiring it.

By this statement is solved the question raised for us by the heretics—whether Adam was formed perfect or imperfect. They ask us: "But, on the one hand, if he was imperfect, how was the work of a perfect God—and above all man—imperfect? And, if he was perfect, how did he disobey the commandments?"

For they also shall hear from us that he was not perfect at his creation, but was fit for taking up virtue.

Clement deals with the same problem in a section of book four of the *Stromateis* by employing an idea from the writings of Plato to assert:

in coming into being he attained perfection and was justified by obedience; this was being brought to maturity with respect to that which depended on him; and the cause was in his choosing, and still more in choosing what was forbidden; God was not the cause....[18]

In these passages Clement tenders his answer to the Valentinians and other "heretics" who thought that sin entered the world because the first man was made in an imperfect manner by the Creator. These people had asked Clement and his fellow Christians to explain how Adam could have been created perfectly if he committed sin after being made, or how the Creator can be perfect if the man whom he made was imperfect. Clement responds to his opponents by arguing that Adam was not perfect when he was created, though the man was made in such a way that he was capable of attaining moral perfection through the exercise of his own free will. Therefore, Adam became morally perfect and was justified after his creation when he finally chose to obey the commandments of God. Through obedience Adam achieved moral maturity as a human being because he chose to make his will conform to that of the Creator. According to Clement, the real cause of sin is not the Creator, as his opponents claim, but human beings, like Adam, who choose to do what is wrong.

The problem of human nature occupies Clement again in the *Stromateis* as he expresses his objections to the Valentinian teaching about the three races of humankind. Just below his discussion of the three races mentioned in the *Preaching of Peter*, Clement says:

at any rate, from the Greek learning, but also from the law, those who admit faith are gathered into the one race of the saved people. It is not that the three peoples are separated in time so someone might assume three natures; but they are instructed in different covenants by the one Lord....[19]

Through such statements Clement repudiates certain Valentinians, like

Heracleon, for claiming that there are three kinds of human beings who are distinguished from each other by nature and in time. Clement insists that the Valentinians are mistaken because all Jews and Greeks who believe in Jesus Christ have become part of the one race of saved people—the Christians. Consequently, the Jews, Greeks, and Christians are only different in that God has given each one of them a unique covenant at a specific point in time so that he might eventually bring them all to salvation.

Clement conducts a polemic against the Valentinians in another one of his writings by adopting some of their language in the *Excerpta* concerning the power of fate. In a section of the *Eclogae Propheticae*, Clement combines a statement from the Valentinians with part of a verse from the Iliad to state:

> as spiritual bodies, which have dealings with and are controlled by the angels set over them, the stars are not the cause of the production of things, but signs of what is taking place and will take place and has taken place in the case of atmospheric changes, fruitfulness and barrenness, pestilence and fevers, and men.
>
> Even in a dream "the stars (τὰ ἄστρα) do not (οὐδ᾽) exert influences (τὰς ἐνεργείας ποιεῖ), but indicate" (σημαίνει δε) "the things that are and that shall be and that have been."[20]

The remarks above show that Clement has borrowed some of the language of the Valentinians in the *Excerpta*, namely, the words: "the stars (τὰ ἄστρα) do not (οὐδ᾽) exert influences (τὰς ἐνεργείας ποιεῖ), but indicate" (δε σημαίνει) things. Clement, though, revises the meaning of these words in order to correct the Valentinian idea that the heavenly bodies display the control of fate over the lives of human beings. Unlike his opponents, Clement insists that the stars only indicate past, present, and future changes in the climate, seasons, and time for the benefit of nature and humankind. For Clement, the angels of the supreme deity govern the movement of the stars to maintain the order of the natural world, but do not determine the attitude or behavior of human beings.

Clement also attacks the Valentinians for their teachings on the baptism of Jesus by creating a hypothetical dialogue between himself and his opponents in the first book of the *Paedagogus*. Quoting a passage from the Gospel of John, Clement argues:

> at the moment when the Lord was baptized, a voice sounded from heaven as a witness to the beloved, saying: "You are my beloved Son, I have begotten you today." Therefore, let us ask the wise whether Christ was already perfect when he was regenerated today, or—what is most outrageous—was he defective. If the latter were the case, it

would have been necessary for him to learn something more. But it is not likely that he learned even one thing more since he is God. For no one can be a greater logos than the Logos, nor, indeed, can anyone be a greater teacher than the only teacher. Thus even though they are unwilling, shall they not confess that the Logos (who was begotten in perfection by the perfect Father) was perfectly regenerated for the sake of a providential prefiguration? And, if Jesus was perfect, why was the perfect one baptized? They say that the baptism of Jesus was necessary to fulfill the precept belonging to man. Very good, I reply.

Then I ask: "Therefore, was he perfect at the same time as his baptism by John?"

"It is clear that he was."

"Then did he learn anything more from him?"

"No."

"But was he perfected by the washing alone and sanctified by the descent of the Spirit?"

"Such was the case."[21]

The aforegoing passage depicts Clement refuting the Valentinians for believing that Jesus only attained spiritual perfection when he received knowledge after his baptism. Against such an opinion, Clement contends that at the very moment when Jesus was baptized, a voice spoke from heaven and bore witness to the fact that he was the beloved son of God, thereby inferring that he was perfect or had complete knowledge of the Father. Indeed, if Jesus had not been perfect in his knowledge of God, he would have had to learn something more after being baptized. But Jesus could not have needed further instruction about the divine because he himself was the word of God and the supreme teacher of human beings. Naturally, then, no one could teach Jesus anything, for he was the source of all knowledge, especially that concerning the Father. Since Jesus was begotten in perfection from the very beginning, he was only made "perfect" or "complete" through baptism in that he was washed in the water and received the Holy Spirit to provide an example for human beings to follow.

Clement reacts to the teachings of the Valentinians about Jesus in another part of his extant works where he endeavors to point out more errors in their soteriology. Drawing upon material from the New Testament in a passage of the *Excerpta*, Clement argues that on account of his humility, the Savior actually appeared in the world with a body of flesh and not in the form of an angel. When the Savior appeared in glory to his disciples on the mountain, he did not do it for the sake of personal glory, but to give the members of the church a clear picture of what life will be like in the heavenly realm. Accordingly, the Savior was the light from above and no less powerful on earth than in heaven. In fact, the Savior was not separated into two beings—one in heaven and one on earth—and he did not leave heaven when he came down as Jesus Christ; for he was the power of the Father and with the supreme deity, everywhere and at all times. Besides, the Savior appeared in full glory to Peter, James, and John so that he might fulfill his own prediction: "There are some of those standing here who shall not taste death until they see the son of man" in glory.[22]

Responding perhaps to an objection from the Valentinians, Clement contends that the disciples were frightened by the voice from heaven and not by the transfigured body of Jesus because their ears were more incredulous than their eyes. In this way the disciples were unlike John the Baptist, who was accustomed to experiencing things on a spiritual plane and so was not frightened by the heavenly voice which he heard at the baptism of Jesus. At any rate, out of concern for the general weakness of human beings, the Lord instructed his disciples not to tell anyone about what they saw or heard on the mountain. Otherwise, the testimony of the disciples might have frightened people and caused them to turn away in disbelief. To be sure, even Peter, James, and John did not see the transfigured Lord with their physical eyes by virtue of the fact that there is no relationship between the bodies of human beings and the spiritual light manifested by the Savior. The disciples were only able to see the light of the Savior because the latter strengthened their eyes, empowering them to perceive what is usually apprehended by the mind alone.[23]

The disciples also were told not to reveal what they saw on the mountain to keep evil persons from discovering the true identity of the Savior. If these people had found out who the Savior was, they would not have crucified him, and the divine plan of salvation for the human race would have remained incomplete. Clement concludes that the disciples must have heard the voice on the mountain since it confirmed what they already believed about the Savior; but those at the baptism of Jesus (except for John) did not hear the heavenly voice because they did not believe that Jesus was the Christ and were still concerned with obeying the commandments of the Jewish law.[24] In short, Clement contradicts the dualism and docetism of the Valentinian Christology by arguing that the Savior, Jesus Christ, was able to come down to earth in the flesh and be with God in heaven at the same time. Unlike his opponents, Clement further contends that the Savior concealed his identity from certain people to ensure that he would be crucified and so bring about the salvation of the human race.

Clement turns his attention to some sayings of the Savior in a subsequent passage of the *Excerpta* to register his opposition to the teaching of the Valentinians on the nature of those who are elect and those who are called. After citing the opinion of the Valentinians about the elect seed, Clement takes up material from a number of places in the canonical gospels to assert:

> the faith is not one, but various. At all events, the Savior said: "Let it be done according to your faith".
>
> Whence it is said that some men of the calling shall be deceived at the appearance of the Antichrist; but this is impossible for "the elect" (τοὺς ἐκλεκτούς); wherefore he said: And "if it were possible," my "elect."
>
> Again, when he says: "Go from the house of my Father": he speaks to "the called" (τοῖς κλητοῖς). In the same way, by the one who came from a foreign land and had consumed his possessions—for whom he killed the fatted calf—he speaks of the called; and where the king called those on the roads into the wedding feast.
>
> On the one hand, all have been called equally; for "he causes it to rain on the just and the unjust", and he makes "the sun" shine upon all. On the other hand, those who have believed to a greater degree are the elect, about whom he says: "No one has seen" my "Father", "except" the Son; "you are the light of the world;" and, "holy Father," sanctify "them in your name".[25]

From the statements above, we can see how Clement has borrowed the Valentinian idea that the Savior used the words "the elect" (τοὺς ἐκλεκτούς) and "the called" (τοῖς κλητοῖς) to represent different types of people in the church. Clement, however, reinterprets the meaning of these words to claim that they refer to people with different levels of faith and in so doing corrects the Valentinian idea that they designate Christians who are spiritual or psychic in nature. To support his argument, Clement describes the Savior teaching people that they will be blessed in proportion to their faith in him. The Savior also revealed that some of the called will be deceived by the Antichrist, but that none of the elect will be led astray due to their superior faith. On other occasions, the Savior pointed out the called by uttering parables about the prodigal son and a wedding feast and by driving the moneychangers from the temple in Jerusalem. Similarly, the Savior identified the elect as the light of the world and those who are sanctified in his name, and he spoke directly to them when he said that no one has seen the Father, except the Son. By way of his remark about God blessing the just and the unjust the Savior further indicated that all human beings are called equally to salvation, though some respond to the call with more faith than others and so are referred to as "the elect". Contrary to the ecclesiology of the Valentinians, Clement argues that the Savior's teaching about the elect and the called proves that members of the church are distinguished from each other by the degree of their faith in God, not by nature.

At a later point in the *Excerpta*, Clement interprets a single statement by the Savior to respond to the Valentinian account of Paul preaching different messages to the psychic and spiritual races. Immediately after citing the Valentinian description of the ministry of Paul, Clement quotes some material from the Gospel of Matthew to claim:

> for each one knows the Lord in their own way, and not all in the same manner. "The angels" "of these little ones" see "the face of the Father"—these little ones who are the elect and who shall be in the same inheritance and perfection. And, probably, the face is both the Son and as much of that comprehensible part of the Father as they see who are taught by the Son; but the rest of the Father is unknown.

Clearly, in this brief passage, Clement has taken over the Valentinian idea of the elect having more knowledge of the Savior than the called, both on earth and in heaven. Despite the fact that he has borrowed this idea from the Valentinians, Clement contends that the Savior's statement about the little ones demonstrates how the elect and the first-created angels will only see the Son or face of the Father in heaven, and therefore, some aspect of the supreme deity will remain unknown to all, except the Son. In so doing Clement contradicts the Valentinians' belief that the elect and their male angels will see the Father directly in the heavenly realm and will have complete knowledge of him since they are spiritual in nature. According to Clement, the elect and the first-created angels are different from the Father in nature or essence and so will only know the supreme deity in part by contemplating the Son in the heavenly realm.[26]

In a passage of the *Eclogae Propheticae*, Clement borrows another idea from the Valentinians in the *Excerpta* to amend the teachings of the latter regarding the human soul. With material drawn from the canonical gospels and the letters of Paul, Clement says:

> when we were earthly, we were Caesar's. And Caesar is the temporal ruler, whose earthly image is also the old man into which he has returned. Therefore, we must render to him the earthly things, which we have borne in "the image of the earthly", and "to God" "the things of God"; for each one of the passions is just like a letter and stamp and sign upon us. Now the Lord impresses upon us another stamp and other names and letters—faith instead of unbelief, and so forth. Thus we are brought from material to spiritual things and bear "the image of the heavenly."[27]

It is apparent from the aforegoing remarks that Clement has appropriated the Valentinian idea of the Savior interpreting the coin given to him for taxes as a symbol of the human soul. But, as he has done in other parts of his writing,

Clement revises this idea to repudiate the Valentinian assertion that the soul possessed by the Devil is filled with evil spirits while the one belonging to God contains an element of the divine. In contrast to the Valentinians, Clement explains how the soul belongs to the Devil as long as it bears the image of earthly things or the passions. The soul, however, is able to transfer its ownership over to God once it begins to bear the image of the things in heaven, that is, when it becomes spiritually pure. This state of purity is achieved by the soul expressing faith in Jesus Christ, ridding itself of the passions, and receiving the Holy Spirit during baptism. A soul such as this turns away from material things and focuses instead on the things of the spiritual world. For Clement, unlike his Valentinian opponents, the Savior's statement about the coin shows how the soul of every human being can be saved by becoming faithful, impassible, and full of spiritual power.

Lastly, in the eighth book of the *Hypotyposes*, Clement borrows a notion from the Valentinians in order to counter their claim about having exclusive possession of the knowledge revealed by the Savior. Alluding to some passages in the canonical gospels, Clement argues that after his resurrection, the Lord imparted knowledge to James the Just, John, and Peter. These three delivered the teachings of the Savior to the other apostles, who then passed it on to Barnabas and the rest of the seventy commissioned by the Lord. Here, without admitting it, Clement has adopted the Valentinian idea of the Savior giving knowledge to his disciples after the resurrection. Ostensibly, Clement has done this to suggest that he and his fellow Christians, rather than the Valentinians, have inherited the true teachings or knowledge given by the Savior. This observation is borne out by the fact that in other parts of his extant writings Clement explains how his own Christian community, and not that of the Valentinians, preserves the teachings delivered by the Savior to the apostles and thence to subsequent generations in the church.[28]

Notes

[1] *Strom.* 4.161.2–62.1 (2.319.21-20.4); on "depart into peace" see Mark 5.34; Luke 8.48; on Melchizedek, the king of Salem, in connection with "righteousness" and "peace" see Heb. 7.1ff.; cf. Gen. 14.18ff.. See also *Strom.* 5.74.3-4 (2.376.2-5) where Clement infers that Basilides' opinion concerning the uniqueness of the world is correct, though his notion of there being more than one deity is not; cf. Iren. *Adv. Haer.* 1.24.3f..

[2] *Strom.* 2.37.1–38.3 (2.132.17–33.13). On the "fear of the Lord" see Ps. 110.10; on the definitions of terror and fear in this passage see Chrysipp. *Fr. Mor.* 411; 416 Arnim; Arist. *Top.* 4.5 (4.5.14ff.) cited in Stählin, *Clemens Alexandrinus,* vol. 2, p. 132; on "the beginning of wisdom" see Ps. 110.10. Note also that Clement is incorrect in his claim that the Basilideans called the Ruler "the greatest" deity. In fact, the Basilideans referred to him as "the Great Ruler" to underscore his inferiority in comparison to the supreme deity.

[3] *Strom.* 2.38.3–5 (2.133.13–24). On "according to the image" see Gen. 1.26. Note that in *Strom.* 2.38.5 (2.133.24) the original reading of "which" (ὅ) in *L* is retained here; cf. Mondésert and Camelot, edd., *Les Stromates: Stromate II,* p. 37. There seems to be no need to change the original text in order to make sense of the passage in question.

[4] *Strom.* 2.74.1-75.2 (2.152.6–23); cf. *Strom.* 2.77.4 (2.153.17f.). On "is rich in mercy" see Eph. 2.4; on the word "being estranged" or "alienated" (ἀπηλλοτριωμένων) see Eph. 2.12; 4.18; Col. 1.21; on the natural affection of parents for their young see Diodorus Siculus 4.44 cited in Stählin, *Clemens Alexandrinus,* vol. 2, p. 152; on the children of God being born as a result of God's will see John 1.12f.. Note that "nothing" (μὴ ὄντων) refers to the pre-existent stuff which, according to some Greek philosophers, was that from which the visible world was created. This "stuff" was thought to have been in a relative state of non-being because it was without quality or form. On the latter see the pertinent remarks in Chadwick, *Early Christian Thought and the Classical Tradition,* pp. 46f. and "Clement of Alexandria," *The Cambridge History of Later Greek and Early Medieval Philosophy,* p. 171.

[5] *Strom.* 4.91.2 (2.288.12ff.).

[6] *Strom.* 4.91.2–3 (2.288.14–9). On Christ destroying death see 2 Tim. 1.10; cf. Heb. 2.14.

[7] *Strom.* 4.91.3–92.2 (2.288.19–29).

[8] *Strom.* 6.71.2–3 (2.467.9–15); cf. Or. *Cels.* 7.13. On Valentinus's idea about the Savior's special body see *Strom.* 3.59.3 (2.223.12–6). It is clear that in this passage Clement has borrowed the notion of the Savior's special body from Valentinus. This is the case because Valentinus is the only writer cited by Clement who expresses such an idea, and Clement only claims the idea as his own in book six of the *Stromateis* after attributing it to Valentinus in book three of the same work.

[9] *Exc.* 30.1, 2; 31.1. Note that in *Strom.* 5.81.3-4 (2.380.12ff.) Clement mentions the Valentinians referring to the bosom of God as "the Depth" because it is unseen and inexpressible. Clement, however, does not say that he approves of "the Depth" as a name for God, nor does he include the term among the good names for God that he lists in *Strom.* 5.81.5–82.2 (2.380.20–81.1). In part of the last passage Clement

says: "Even if we name it as we incorrectly call it either the One or the Good or Mind or Absolute Being or Father or God or Creator or Lord, we do not speak as if we are supplying its name; but being at a loss, we use good names, so that the mind might have these to lean upon and not be misled about other things."

[10] *Exc.* 8.1, 2-4. On "in the bosom of the Father" see John 1.18; on the one who explained "the bosom of the Father" see John 1.18; on the "First-born of all creation" see Col. 1.15; on the light see John 1.4; on "the darkness did not overcome" him see John 1.5. See also *Exc.* 7.3-4 where Clement makes the same argument as in *Exc.* 8 while appropriating the Valentinian term "Pleroma" (Πλήρωμα) as a designation for the heavenly realm; cf. *Exc.* 21.3; 22.4; 23.2 passim. The word "pleroma" is also used in Col. 1.19 and 2.9, though not as a name for the heavenly world as in the Valentinian material of the *Excerpta.*

[11] *Exc.* 19.1-20.1. On "the Logos became flesh" see John 1.14; on "in the beginning" see John 1.1; on "what came into being in him" see John 1.3f.; on "put on the new man" see Eph. 4.24; on "he who is an image" and "First-born of all creation" see Col. 1.15; on "by him" see Col. 1.16; on "he took the form of a slave" see Phil. 2.7; on "I have begotten you before the morning star" see Psalms 109.3; on the words "name" and "before the sun" see Psalms 71.17. Note that in later church history the use of the term "First-created" was abandoned; cf. Sagnard, *Extr. de Théod.*, p. 97 n.3. In the present passage Clement simply wants to say that when the Logos comes forth from the Father as the Son, the unity of the divine substance is not affected; cf. Casey, *Exc. ex Theod.*, p. 114. It should also be noted that the word "son" (υἱός) in the phrase "son of the Logos in its identity" is a conjecture in Stählin, *Clemens Alexandrinus*, vol. 3, p. 113 and Sagnard, *Extr. de Théod.*, p. 95. The word "logos" rather than "son" is admitted in the same phrase by Casey in *Exc. ex Theod.*, p. 54. Regardless of whether "son" or "logos" is correct in *Exc.* 19.4, Clement means that the Logos is one being, but it has two stages in its existence: 1) when it is the Logos in its identity or mind of God; and 2) when it is the "son" of the Logos in its identity or the Only-begotten Son and instrument of creation. On these stages of the Logos see Wolfson, *The Philosophy of the Church Fathers*, pp. 204–17, 269; Lilla, *Clement of Alexandria*, pp. 200ff..

[12] Clement certainly discusses his own ideas in the *Excerpta* in order to show how the teachings of the Valentinians therein are incorrect. This is demonstrated by the fact that whenever Clement directly addresses the Valentinians in the *Excerpta*, he criticizes them; see e.g. *Exc.* 1.3; 8.1-4; 17.2-4; 24.2. Clement's remarks in *Exc.* 7.3-4 and 9.1-12.3 also appear to have been intended as a polemic against the Valentinians since the material in *Exc.* 7 parallels that in *Exc.* 8, just as the statements in *Exc.* 9-12 form a single piece of work with the critical comments in *Exc.* 8. Clement's statements in *Exc.* 19-20 must have been a further part of this polemic because they pick up and extend the argument begun in *Exc.* 8. Even when Clement does not say explicitly that he is responding to the teachings of the Valentinians, he discusses the same subjects as them but in terms that are different from theirs. Thus Clement seems to have expressed his own ideas on the Savior, the elect, and the ascent into the heavenly realm in *Exc.* 4-5, 23.4-5, and 27.1-6 in opposition to the opinions of the Valentinians in *Exc.* 1.1, 23.2-3, and 26.1-3. Given these observations, I have treated almost all of the Clementine passages in the *Excerpta* as a polemic against the Valentinians. I have not included *Exc.* 13-15 and 18 in my exposition, however, for it is not clear how Clement's statements in these passages are directed against the Valentinians. It is possible that Clement

wanted to use his ideas on the heavenly bread, the demons, the human soul, and the righteous in *Exc.* 13-15 and 18 against the Valentinian teachings recorded in *Exc.* 58-9, 48, 50-1, and 37; but the unfinished nature of the *Excerpta* prevents us from knowing this for certain. Note that a similar evaluation of the Clementine portions of the *Excerpta* is given in Casey, *Exc. ex Theod.*, pp. 25-33. I also agree with Casey that the material in the *Excerpta* was intended for inclusion in another book of the *Stromateis;* see *Exc. ex Theod.*, p. 30. Indeed, the material in the *Excerpta* fulfills some of Clement's promise in *Strom.* 4.3.2-4 (2.249.11-6) to discuss and refute the tenets of the heretics regarding theology and cosmology.

13 *Exc.* 33.2. On the "First-born" see Col. 1.15, 18; on the Savior as the "head" see Col. 1.18; cf. Eph. 1.22; 4.15; on the church as the fruit of the Savior see Rom. 7.4; cf. Polyc. *Ep.* 1.2.

14 *Exc.* 8.2; 10.3–4. On "all things were made by him" see John 1.3; on the seven see the seven holy angels in *Tobit* 12.15 and the seven spirits in Is. 11.2-3; Zech. 4.10; Rev. 5.6.

15 *Exc.* 11.4-12.3. On the ministry of the first-created see also *Ecl.* 56.7 (3.153.20ff.); 57.1–2 (3.153.25-8); on the seven or first-created as the highest angels see also *Strom.* 6.143.1 (1.504.18f.); on the terms "archangels" and "angel" see 1 Thess. 4.16; Jude 9; Matt. 1.20; 2.13, 19 et al; Philo *De Conf. Ling.* 146; *Quis Rer. Div. Her.* 205; *De Somn.* 1.157; 190 et al; on "the face of the Father" which is beheld by the angels see Matt. 18.10; on the hierarchy of divine beings in the heavenly realm see Rev. 4.4, 6f.; 5.6, 11; 8.2; cf. *Exc.* 10.1-3; 11.2-3; on "into which angels desire to gaze" see 1 Pet. 1.12; on "unapproachable light" see 1 Tim. 6.16; on a "power of God" see 1 Cor. 1.24. I have not discussed the material in *Exc.* 10.1-3, 5-6 and 11.1-3 because it adds nothing to the general argument, namely, that Clement presents his own views on the nature of the heavenly beings as a corrective to those of the Valentinians. In these passages Clement describes how the Son and the various angels have their own form, figure, shape, and body, and how these characteristics differ according to the rank of each being in the heavenly realm. Clement also argues that the heavenly beings must have bodies and forms so that they can be seen by each other, but that their bodies do not have any gender like those of earthly beings.

16 *Exc.* 12.1; 10.6; 23.4, 5; 27.3. On the face or beginning of the vision of the Father see Matt. 18.10; on the Son as the one who alone knows the Father see Matt. 11.27; John 1.18; cf. *Strom.* 1.178.2–79.1 (2.109.27ff.); 5.81.3 (2.380.10ff.).

17 *Strom.* 6.141.7–42.2 (2.504.2–7). On the rest of God and "as some suppose" see Aristobolus cited in Eus. *P.E.* 13.12.11; on "God doing" see Philo *Leg. All.* 1.5; on the idea that the Creator can only do what is best because he is good see Plato *Tim.* 30a; on "the arrangement" and "for all time" see Aristobolus cited in Eus. *P.E.* 13.12.11; on the things created being brought into order out of disorder (ἀταξία) see Plato *Tim.* 30a; cf. Philo *De Somn.* 1.241.

18 *Strom.* 6.95.5-96.2 (2.480.3-11); 4.150.4 (2.315.8–11). On the one who chooses being the cause see Plato *Rep.* 10.617e.

19 *Strom.* 6.42.2–3 (2.452.24–8). On the idea of three peoples or races see fragment 2 of the *Keryg. Petri* cited in *Strom.* 6.41.6–7 (2.452.17f.); on the Valentinian doctrine of the three races based on three natures see *Exc.* 54.1–3; 56.2f.; on the three races being separated in time see the teaching of Heracleon mentioned in Origen *In Joh.* 13.16 in Foerster, *Gnosis*, vol. 1, p. 171.

[20] *Ecl.* 55.1-2 (3.152.14-9). On certain angels being set over and controlling the stars see Herm. *Vis.* 3.4.1; cf. Just. *2 Apol.* 5.2; Athenag. *Leg.* 24.3f.; *1 Enoch* 75.3f.; on the Valentinian statement: "the stars do not exert influences, but indicate": see *Exc.* 70.2 (3.129.22f.); on "the things that are, ..." see *Il.* 1.70. The Valentinians are the most probable source for Clement's remark about the stars not exerting influences because they are the only people cited by him who use such language and there is no evidence that they ever borrowed anything from him. In fact, I think that the material in the *Eclogae Propheticae*, like that in the *Excerpta*, was meant for inclusion in the *Stromateis*. This seems to be the case because the *Eclogae* discusses prophetic teachings on theology and creation—the very teachings which Clement wanted to add to the *Stromateis*, according to his remarks at the beginning of book four; cf. *Strom.* 4.2.2-3 (2.248.19-25); 4.3.3-4 (2.249.13-6).

[21] *Paed.* 1.25.2-3 (1.105.4-18). On "you are my beloved Son" see Ps. 2.7; Heb. 1.5; 5.5. The gospel saying "you are my beloved Son," as quoted by Clement, appears in some ancient manuscripts; see Wood, *Clement of Alexandria: Christ the Educator*, p. 25 n.3. On the Savior not needing to be baptized see also *Ecl.* 7.2 (3.138.27ff.). The Valentinians are clearly the opponents whom Clement addresses in this passage, for they thought that the earthly Jesus needed to be baptized in order to receive the Spirit from above and thus all of the power of the Aeons in the Pleroma; cf. *Exc.* 16; 22.6-7. The Valentinians cited by Clement do not expressly state that Jesus obtained knowledge after his baptism. This, however, is implied by their comments about people imitating Jesus in all things and being liberated from the material world by knowledge acquired after baptism; *Exc.* 76.1; 85.1; 78.1-2; cf. *Exc.* 22.6-7; 59.1; 61.2. On the Valentinian character of Clement's opponents here see also my comments in chap. 4, n.21.

[22] *Exc.* 4.1-3. On the transfiguration see Matt. 17.1-8; Mark 9.2-8; Luke 9.28-36; on the elect race see 1 Pet. 2.9; on the light from above see John 1.8; on manifested in the flesh see 1 Tim. 3.16; on the power of the Father see 1 Cor. 1.24; on "there are some standing here..." see Matt. 16.28; Luke 9.27. Note that Clement, unlike the Valentinians, believes that the Savior possessed a real physical body. Unlike his opponents, Clement also does not portray a psychic and a spiritual Christ and makes no distinction between the Savior and Jesus or the elect race and the rest of the Christian church.

[23] *Exc.* 5.1-3. On the fear of the disciples when they heard the voice see Matt. 17.6; on the voice at Jesus' baptism see Matt. 3.17; Mark 1.11; Luke 3.22; on the Savior instructing the disciples to tell no one see Matt. 17.9; Mark 9.9. What objection might the Valentinians have raised against Clement's doctrine? The Valentinians probably thought that since the disciples were unable to bear the sound of the voice from heaven, they also must have been incapable of perceiving the spiritual nature of the Savior. If this is the case, the Valentinians would quite naturally have explained the disciples "seeing" the transfigured Savior in a symbolic sense. Clement himself admits that the disciples only witnessed the transfiguration because their eyes were strengthened by the Savior. But, unlike his opponents, Clement does not think that recognition of the Savior's true nature depends upon a person being a member of the spiritual race; on the Valentinian opinion regarding this matter see *Exc.* 23.2-3; cf. 43.1.

[24] *Exc.* 5.4-5.

[25] *Exc.* 9.1-3. On the Valentinian terms "the elect" and "the called" see *Exc.* 1.2;

58.1; cf. *Strom.* 2.10.2-3 (2.118.13-7); on "let it be done..." see Matt. 9.29; on "if it were possible..." see Matt. 24.24; on the term "the calling" or "called" see also Rom. 1.6f.; 8.28; 1 Cor. 1.2, 24; Jude 1; Rev. 17.14; on some of "the called" being lost see Matt. 22.11–4; cf. Matt. 24.24; on going from the Father's house see John 2.16; on killing the fatted calf see Luke 15.23; on the wedding feast see Matt. 22.9; on "he causes it to rain..." see Matt. 5.45; on "no one has seen" my "Father" "except" the Son see John 1.18; 6.46; on "you are the light of the world" see Matt. 5.14; on "holy Father" sanctify "them in your name" see John 17.11, 17. I do not agree with Casey that in this passage the called represent all human beings and the elect those who believe; cf. Casey, *Exc. ex Theod.*, p. 104 n.4. Instead, Clement says that the faith (i.e. the whole church) is not one with respect to belief and that the elect believe more than others, namely, the called.

[26] *Exc.* 23.4-5. On each knowing in their own way see *Ecl.* 57.2-3 (3.153.28-54.2); on the quotations see Matt. 18.10; on the different ranks of the elect and the called in heaven see *Ecl.* 56.3-5 (3.153.8-13); 57.4-5 (3.154.5-13); cf. *Strom.* 6.107.2-108.3 (2.485.24-86.11); 6.114.1-4 (2.489.6-15); 7.7.1 (3.6.29-7.1); 7.13.1 (3.10.6-16). Note also how Clement, unlike the Valentinians, thinks that the elect and the called will be in the same heavenly realm and that the called will be able to purify themselves and become elect even after the death of their physical bodies.

[27] *Ecl.* 24.1–3 (3.143.12–9). On the Valentinian idea about the Savior's interpretation of the coin see *Exc.* 86.1-3; on that which is Caesar's and Caesar as the temporal ruler see Matt. 22.21; Mark 12.16f.; Luke 20.24f.; on the old man see 1 Cor. 15.45f.; on rendering to Caesar and "to God" see Matt. 22.21; Mark 12.17; Luke 20.25; on "the image of the earthly" and "heavenly" see 1 Cor. 15.49.

[28] *Fr.* 13 Stählin (3.199.21-4) in Eus. *H.E.* 2.1.4f.. On the Valentinian idea of the Savior imparting knowledge after the resurrection see *Exc.* 3.1-2; cf. 45.1; 56.2; 59.1; 78.2; on Jesus with his apostles after the resurrection see Matt. 28.16f.; Mark 16.12f.; Luke 24.13f., 36f.; John 20.19f., 26f.; 21.1f.; 1 Cor. 15.5ff.; on the seventy see Luke 10.1, 17; on Clement's claim to have the teaching revealed by the Savior see *Strom.* 6.131.5 (2.498.15-8); 1.11.3-12.1 (2.9.4-8). See also the discussion of *Fr.* 13 in Lilla, *Clement of Alexandria*, p. 159.

4

Clement on the Nature of the Church

The Polemic against Basilides and His Followers

IN the seventh book of the *Stromateis*, Clement brands Basilides as a heretic for attempting to establish his own Christian community long after the foundation of the first church. After discussing the time when Jesus and his apostles conducted their ministries on earth, Clement argues that those who founded the heresies were born during the reign of Hadrian and flourished until the rule of Antoninus the Elder. Clement identifies Basilides as a founder of one of these sects, and he explains how such groups are a deformation of the original church since they came into being so long after the time of the Lord. A little further on Clement suggests that the followers of Basilides are not part of the true church because they are named after someone other than Jesus Christ. Clement adds that the Basilideans also cannot possess the doctrines of the apostle Matthias as they claim, for the teachings and traditions of all the apostles are identical and do not reflect the differing opinions of the heretics.[1] On the whole, Clement categorizes Basilides as a heretic by asserting that his own Christian community, rather than that of his opponent, is the direct descendant of the original church and thus the sole inheritor of apostolic doctrine.

Near the beginning of the fifth book of the *Stromateis*, Clement also engages in a polemic in which he criticizes the opinions of Basilides on the nature of faith. In the midst of describing Basilides' doctrine of faith Clement relates how his opponent does not say that belief is a power or a rational assent of the free will of the soul. Although Clement does not state this directly, he notes these omissions on the part of Basilides to show how the latter is mistaken in thinking that faith is an innate quality or capacity in the souls of elect persons. For Clement, unlike his opponent, faith is a power produced in the soul of every person who freely and rationally chooses to believe in Jesus Christ.[2]

Just below, in the same section of the *Stromateis*, Clement continues his opposition to Basilides' idea that faith is an exclusive possession of the elect. Quoting some material from the book of Genesis, Clement says:

> the commandments, which are both in the old and in the new covenant, are superfluous then...if someone is faithful and elect by nature, as Basilides thinks; and it would have been possible for nature to shine forth at some time or other even apart from the coming of the Savior. But if they should say that the coming of the Lord was

necessary, the unique characteristics of nature are gone for them, since the elect are saved by instruction, purification, and doing good works, but not by nature. At least then, let them tell us whether Abraham was chosen or not when, through hearing, he believed the voice that promised under the oak in Mamre: I give this land "to you" "and to your seed". But if he was not chosen, how did he believe immediately—by nature, as it were? And if he was chosen, their hypothesis is destroyed because an election is discovered and saved even before the coming of the Lord; for "it was reckoned to him as righteousness."[3]

Clement contends in the passage above that the doctrine of faith held by Basilides eliminates the need for the coming of the Savior and obedience to the commandments in the old and new testaments. Clement explains how Basilides and his followers cannot say that the coming of the Lord was necessary to effect the salvation of humankind, for then they would have to admit that people are saved by being taught, receiving forgiveness of sins, and doing good works, not by their innate capacity to believe. Indeed, if a person's willingness to believe is a sign that they have been chosen for salvation, as Basilides supposes, then the patriarch Abraham must have been elect and saved because he believed so readily in the promise which God gave to him under the tree in Mamre. Under such circumstances, Basilides and his followers cannot claim that the Lord came down to save Abraham and others like him since such people were already saved before the incarnation by virtue of their natural capacity to believe. In short, Clement rejects Basilides' conception of faith because it undermines the value of ethical behavior and the advent of the Savior, Jesus Christ.

Basilides is targeted by Clement for criticism on the same issue concerning the nature of the elect in a passing remark located in book four of the *Stromateis*. There Clement categorically rejects Basilides' statement about the supermundane nature of the elect by explaining how no human being is a stranger in the world because one God created the universe and all people have the same nature—one that is entirely different from that of the divinity. Clement also insists that the elect people or Christians only exist as strangers in the world since they live contingently, knowing that the things acquired on earth will be left behind them at death. In this way Clement condemns Basilides for claiming that the supreme deity is not the creator of the world and that the elect are identified with this deity, but separated from the world and other human beings due to their innate quality of faith. Against these errors, Clement upholds the idea of the absolute unity of God, the inherent equality of humankind, the distinction between divine and human natures, and the basic goodness of the created order.[4]

Clement takes up his attack on Basilides again in the fourth book of the

Stromateis by demonstrating how his opponent's views on martyrdom make God responsible for evil. After quoting Basilides' opinions on how the Christian martyrs suffer to atone for their sins, Clement asks his readers:

> and how can this be true when confessing and being punished or not depends on us? For providence, as held by Basilides, is destroyed in the case of the one who shall deny. Therefore, I shall ask him whether the confessor who is arrested, shall testify and be punished in accordance with providence or not. For the one who denies shall not be punished. But if Basilides shall say that this one must not have needed to be punished because they escaped from martyrdom, he shall bear witness against his own will that the destruction of those who shall deny is from providence. And how can there still be laid up in heaven a very glorious reward for the one who suffered on account of bearing witness? But if providence did not permit the sinner to come to sinning, it is unjust in both cases, both in not rescuing the one who is dragged to punishment for the sake of righteousness, and in rescuing the one who wanted to do wrong—the one who did what he wanted by virtue of his will, but providence prevented the deed and unjustly favored the sinner. And how is he not without the true God when he deifies the Devil and dares to call the Lord a sinful man? For the Devil tempts us because he knows what we are, but he does not know whether we shall endure. Yet, wishing to shake us from the faith and to subject us to himself, he tempts us. This is the only thing which he is permitted: for the sake of saving us from ourselves when we have taken leave of the commandments, for the purpose of shaming the one who has tempted us and failed, for strengthening those in the church, and for the conscience of those who marvel at the endurance. But if martyrdom is a reward through punishment, then both faith and teaching, through which martyrdom comes, are co-workers of punishment—of which what other absurdity could be greater?[5]

With these statements Clement excoriates Basilides' idea that divine providence leads Christians to martyrdom so that they can atone for their sins. Clement argues that the claims of Basilides are wrong because confessing or denying Christ before a court of law actually depends on the free will of each person. In fact, the doctrine of Basilides destroys the notion of providence when one considers the case of a person who chooses to deny Christ. For, in denying their faith before the court, a person is able to escape the suffering of martyrdom which God intended as a punishment for their sins. Yet, even if God prompted someone to deny Christ because they were innocent and did not deserve to suffer, he would still be the cause of the punishment that must eventually befall such a person for lying about their faith.

By way of a rhetorical question Clement also contends that there is no rational justification for God to give the Christian martyrs a glorious reward in heaven if the suffering of the latter is a just punishment meted out for their sins. Under the terms of Basilides' doctrine, God ends up being unjust again when a person who intends to deny Christ is prevented by one thing or another from having to appear in court and answer questions about their faith. In the aforementioned cases God is unjust both in preventing one person from being punished for their intention to commit sin and in allowing another person, who does confess Christ, to suffer for doing what is right.

Reacting to Basilides' assertion that no human being who suffers is truly innocent, Clement accuses his opponent of deifying the Devil and calling Jesus a sinful man. Clement explains how the Devil causes the suffering of the martyrs in an effort to make people deny their faith and obtain power over them, though he has no prior knowledge of whether any given person will deny Christ in the face of persecution. In reality, God only allows the Devil to tempt people with the threat of martyrdom because those who resist this temptation will be saved in spite of their past sins and their endurance will strengthen the faith of others in the church. Similarly, the perseverance of the martyrs demonstrates the Devil's inability to seduce people away from the faith and may lead some of the persecutors to become Christians out of admiration for the courage displayed by their former victims. Clement concludes that if one were to accept the theory of Basilides concerning martyrdom, then the very faith and teachings for which the martyrs are being punished would be the cause of suffering—an idea that is patently absurd.

Further on, in the same section of book four of the *Stromateis*, Clement resumes his argument against Basilides' teachings on martyrdom. Setting up a series of questions to point out flaws in the logic of his opponent, Clement asks the members of his audience:

> again, where is faith in retribution for the sins committed before martyrdom happens? Where is the love for God that is persecuted and endures for the truth? Where is praise for the one who has confessed or censure for the one who has denied? And again, of what use is right conduct—mortifying the desires and hating none of the things in creation? But if, as Basilides himself says, we suppose that one part of the declared will of God is to love all things, ...a second is to desire nothing, and a third is to hate nothing, punishment shall also be by the will of God—a thing which is impious to think. For neither did the Lord suffer by the will of the Father, nor are those who are persecuted, persecuted by the will of God; since one of two things is

the case: either the persecution on account of the will of God is a good thing, or those who issue the decrees and afflict the martyrs are guiltless. But nothing occurs without the will of the Lord of the universe. Indeed, it remains to say briefly that such things happen when God has not prevented them; for this alone preserves both the providence and the goodness of God. Therefore, we must not think that God produces afflictions (far be it from us to think this!); rather we must be persuaded that he does not prevent those who contrive them and uses up the shameless acts of those who oppose him for a good purpose. Accordingly, he says: "I shall tear down the wall" "and it shall be for trampling underfoot": because providence is such an educative art—in the case of others, for the sins belonging to each one, and in the case of the Lord and his apostles, for our sins.... So, on account of this—our sanctification—the Lord was not prevented from suffering. Therefore, if one of them were to say in defense that the martyr is punished for the sins committed before this embodiment and that he shall leave behind again the fruit of his conduct in this life— for so the administration is arranged—we shall ask him if the retribution is produced by providence. For if the retribution is not from the divine administration, the dispensation of purifications is gone and their hypothesis has fallen. But if the purifications are from providence, the punishments are as well. And even if providence begins to be moved because of the Ruler, as they say, yet it is implanted in substances at the same time as the creation of those substances by the God of the universe. This being the case, they must confess either that the punishment is not unjust (and those who condemn and persecute the martyrs act rightly), or that the persecutions are produced by the will of God. No longer, then, do pain and fear, as they say, come into existence with things, like rust with iron; but they are added to the soul as a result of its own will.[6]

Through these statements Clement reopens his polemic against Basilides by showing how his opponent's theory of martyrdom undermines the value of confessing Christ in the courts of law. Clement infers that there is no justification for praising those who confess Christ or censuring those who deny him if confession and denial are actions determined by God. In fact, there is no reason for people to perform any good deed, including the elimination of passions from their souls, if God is the one who causes them to act. The truth is, Basilides is guilty of impiety when he says that God wills the suffering of the martyrs; for God is no more responsible for their suffering than the crucifixion of Jesus. If the hypothesis of Basilides were true, one would have to admit that persecution is good (though it is really evil), or that persecution is evil, but the judges and executioners are not guilty of doing wrong because their actions are determined by God. In opposition to the latter premises Clement affirms that the concept of divine goodness and providence is only defensible when one assumes that God allows, but does not cause the suffering of the martyrs.

Clement supports the aforegoing idea about divine providence by explaining that God allows the martyrs to suffer so he can turn the evil actions of the persecutors toward a good end—the salvation of people. The prophet Isaiah illustrated this principle by describing how a farmer employs cattle to clear the weeds from his vineyard and thus enable the existing vines to increase in size and provide room for new vines to be planted. Likewise, God uses the destructive acts of the persecutors to strengthen and increase the membership of the church. Such a transformation of evil into good is effected primarily through a process of education in which the sight of the suffering martyrs convicts the consciences of the persecutors, leading some of them to repent of their sins and become Christians. This is the way in which the souls of the martyrs were convicted of sin as they heard about the suffering of Jesus and his apostles for the first time. Therefore, it is obvious that Jesus was only allowed to suffer because God knew that that would bring people to a new way of pure and holy living.

Drawing his argument on martyrdom to a close, Clement repeats his assertion that the Basilideans must abandon their hypothesis about the Christian martyrs being punished for their sins or admit that they consider God to be the cause of all suffering. If God does not ordain martyrdom as a just punishment for wrongdoing, then Christians cannot atone for their sins by suffering as martyrs and the Basilidean doctrine of atonement is proven to be false. But if God has established martyrdom as a penalty for sin, then the Basilideans have made the deity responsible for suffering. Furthermore, even the doctrine of the Ruler espoused by the Basilideans blames the suffering of the martyrs on God, for it claims that the supreme deity determined the nature and course of everything in the universe from the very moment of creation. Clement ends by arguing that the Basilideans are also incorrect for saying that pain and fear are endemic to human nature since the fact of the matter is that people freely choose to let the various passions into their souls. Consequently, Clement rejects the doctrine of martyrdom held by Basilides and his followers because it makes God the cause of human nature and everything that is evil, including the persecution of Christians.

Clement returns to his polemic against Basilides regarding the purpose of suffering in one other short passage of book four of the *Stromateis*. Following his citation of Basilides' doctrine on the forgiveness of sins, Clement quotes a verse from the Psalms to state:

...he speaks as if some man, rather than God, supplies such a gift. To him, the scripture says: "You thought, lawless one, that I would be like you." But if we are punished for voluntary things, we are punished not so that those things which are done may be undone, but because they were done. And punishment does not help the one who has sinned by undoing his sin, but that he may sin no longer, and, indeed, that another person may not fall into the same things. Therefore, the good God chastises for these three reasons: first, so that he who is chastised may become better than himself; then, so that those who can be saved through example may be prevented from sinning by being warned; and thirdly, so that the one who is injured may not be easily despised and be apt to suffer harm again. And there are two methods of correction: the one instructive and the other punitive, which we have also called corrective. One must know only that those who fall into sin after the washing of baptism are those who are disciplined; for the things which were practiced first are forgiven, but the things which come into being afterwards are cleansed.[7]

Basilides is criticized by Clement in this passage for saying that sins committed involuntarily or in ignorance before baptism are forgiven while those done afterwards must be redeemed through suffering. Clement argues that the kind of forgiveness envisioned by his opponent is more like that of a human being than God. Contrary to the claims of Basilides, God does not chastise people for sins committed after baptism in order to erase the fact that such things have been done, but to prevent the guilty person from making the same mistake again. Like a father or a teacher, God chastises people for their sins after baptism so they will amend their behavior in the future, other persons will not fall into the same error, and the victims of sin will escape any further injury. To accomplish these ends, God uses two methods: instruction before baptism for those who are ignorant of right and wrong, and chastisement after the washing of redemption for those who continue to sin despite their knowledge of the divine commandments. According to Clement, God's sole purpose in chastising people is to educate and discipline them.

As he has done in the case of the founder of their community, Clement opposes the opinions of the Basilideans about faith as a natural quality or capacity within elect persons. In the second book of the *Stromateis*, Clement responds to the Basilidean doctrine of faith by saying:

therefore, faith is no longer a right exercise of free choice, if it is an advantage of nature; nor shall the unbeliever receive a just reward, since he is not the cause of his unbelief, as the believer is not the cause of his faith. But if we are to think correctly, the whole character

and difference of faith and unbelief cannot fall under either praise or
blame because they have natural necessity as an antecedent—necessity
which is produced by the power of the Almighty. And if we are drawn
by the puppet-strings of natural influence, like inanimate things, both
the voluntary and involuntary act, and impulse their guide, are
superfluous. And I, at least, no longer consider that a living being
whose appetite is under the dominion of necessity when it is moved by
an external cause. And again, where is there any place for the
repentance of the unbeliever, through which the forgiveness of sin
comes? So that baptism is no longer reasonable, nor the blessed seal,
nor the Son, nor the Father; but God, I think, is discovered to be the
distributor of natures to us—something which does not have voluntary
faith as the foundation of salvation.[8]

Clement explains in these remarks how there is no justification for praising
a person who believes, or censuring one who does not, if faith is given to
certain people by God instead of chosen through an exercise of free will. The
very idea that human beings possess a faculty of free will is rendered
meaningless by the Basilidean doctrine of faith, for anyone whose choices are
determined by an external source is not really functioning as a living being.
The Basilidean notion of faith also undermines the Christian scheme of
salvation because it assumes that some people are saved by nature and not by
repentance, forgiveness, baptism, and other things which are commanded by
God through Jesus Christ. In this situation God becomes responsible for
human nature, and salvation no longer depends on a person's decision to believe
or otherwise. Subsequently, in another section of book two, Clement describes
how hope is engendered by faith, inferring thereby that the Basilideans are
mistaken in their claim that hope as well as faith is an innate quality of the
elect person. Unlike his opponents, Clement maintains that every Christian's
hope of acquiring salvation originates with and is built upon the faith which
they have freely chosen.[9]

At the beginning of book three of the *Stromateis*, Clement picks up his
attack on the Basilidean doctrine of nature in relationship to the question of
Christian marriage. Immediately after citing statements made by Isidore and his
fellow Basilideans on marriage, Clement quotes material from several passages
in the letters of Paul to assert:

I have set these opinions before you to refute those Basilideans who do
not live properly, supposing either that they have the power even to
commit sin because of their perfection, or because they shall be saved
completely by nature due to their innate election even if they sin now.
Even the forefathers of their doctrines do not agree to do the same

things as them! Therefore, do not let those who slip in under the name of Christ, and who live more intemperately than the most unrestrained among the pagans, inflict blasphemy on the name; "for such are false apostles and deceitful workers," "whose end shall be like their works." Consequently, continence is a disregard for the body in accordance with the confession to God. For continence is not only engaged in the case of sexual matters, but also in other things which the soul wrongly desires when it is not satisfied with the necessities. And there is also a continence concerning the tongue, property, use, and desire. But continence does not only teach us to practice self-control; indeed, it grants self-control to us since it is a power and a divine grace. So when we teach those among us about what lies ahead, we must say that we deem blessed the state of sexual abstinence and whoever has been given this by God; yet we also honor monogamy and the dignity of one marriage, saying that it is necessary to suffer with and "bear the burdens of one another", lest anyone "who thinks that he stands" well should "fall." And with regard to a second marriage, the apostle said: If you burn, marry.[10]

Here Clement shows how the marital practices of some Basilideans stand in direct contrast to the teachings of their predecessors, Isidore and his fellows. These newer members of the Basilidean community seem to have indulged in libertine marital and sexual practices because they thought that they were destined for salvation as a result of their innate capacity or quality of faith. Clement, however, believes that these Basilideans are more morally corrupt than their pagan neighbors, and he demands that they refrain from calling themselves "Christians" so their actions will not bring the name of the Lord into disrepute among unbelievers. According to Clement, these libertines are the people whom Paul referred to when he spoke about "false apostles" and "deceitful workers" who will be destroyed along with their evil deeds.

Reflecting on his own opinions about marriage, Clement explains how continence is a general disregard for the desires of the physical body and should be practiced by every Christian in accordance with their faith in God. Christians are obligated to practice self-control in matters of sex, speech, the acquisition and use of property, and the desire for anything which is not necessary to sustain physical life. This ability to exercise self-control is given to people through the grace of God and strengthened by continuous practice. Therefore, the church considers celibacy to be a blessed state for those who have the ability to remain continent, but upholds the dignity of one marriage for those who desire sexual relations. The church also believes that Christians must bear the burdens of their brothers and sisters to keep one another from falling into sin. It is for this reason that the apostle Paul enjoins members of the church to marry a second time if they want to continue having sexual relations after the death of their first marriage partner. Thus Clement indirectly expresses approval of some of the ideas about marriage that were taught by Isidore and certain other Basilideans. This enables Clement to condemn the libertine Basilideans for transgressing the doctrines of Jesus, Paul, and their own teachers, and thereby, exposing the church to ridicule from its pagan opponents.

Clement makes a final argument against the Basilideans by declaring his opposition to those who believe in the transmigration of the soul. In a passage of the *Eclogae Propheticae*, Clement contends that we are made by God and have not existed before this present life, and that if we had a prior existence, we ought to know where we were and how and why we have come hither. Clement's point is simply that if reincarnation were a fact, then the Basilideans and others would not have to teach people about it because everyone would already have knowledge of such things through their own experience. In contrast to his opponents Clement insists that God gives each human being one body and allows them to come into the world one time.[11]

The Polemic against Valentinus

Valentinus becomes the object of Clement's polemic in a portion of book seven of the *Stromateis* where he is categorized as a heretic along with Basilides and others. Clement says that Valentinus is a sectarian and a teacher of false doctrine because he created his own religious community long after Jesus established the original church. In addition, Clement infers that the followers of Valentinus are not members of the true church since they have taken their name from someone other than Jesus Christ. As with Basilides, Clement makes the aforegoing assertions so he and his fellow Christians can lay exclusive claim to being members of the one true church founded by the Lord.[12]

The beginning of book five of the *Stromateis* also provides Clement with an occasion to refute Valentinus on the question of whether people are destined for salvation because of their spiritual nature, or not. With the same argument that he uses against the concept of faith espoused by Basilides, Clement explains how a person cannot be saved by obedience to the commandments of the old and new testaments, or by being forgiven for their sins and living in a morally upright way, if, as Valentinus says, they are guaranteed salvation on the basis of their spiritual nature. This hypothesis further destroys the need for the salvific work of Jesus Christ by suggesting that some people, like the patriarch Abraham, were saved long before the incarnation. In effect, Clement finds Valentinus's doctrine of salvation by nature completely unacceptable since it contradicts his own belief in the reality of free will and negates the value of the ethics and soteriology taught by the Christian church.[13]

In book two of the *Stromateis*, Clement repudiates the opinions of Valentinus once more, this time in regard to the nature of the human soul. Quoting Valentinus's description of evil spirits dwelling in the soul, Clement says:

> let them tell us, then, what is the cause of such a soul not being cared for from the beginning. For either it is not worthy (and how can providence come to it, except by repentance?), or there is a nature which is saved, as he maintains. And it is necessary that this—which is cared for from the beginning because of its kinship—provide no entrance for the unclean spirits, unless it is hard-pressed and proves to be weak. For if he grants that it chose better things after it repented, he shall say, unwillingly, the very thing which the truth teaches us: that salvation is produced by a change of obedience, but not by nature.[14]

Clement demonstrates with these statements how Valentinus contradicts himself by claiming that the soul of every person is inhabited by evil spirits and that souls containing a spiritual element are set free of these demons by the power of God. Clement asks Valentinus and his followers to explain why God does not prevent the demons from entering a soul with the spiritual element when that soul is first created. On the one hand, the Valentinians cannot argue that such a soul is too sinful to receive divine protection from the beginning, for then they would have to admit that it does not become worthy of God's care because of the spiritual element in it, but by virtue of its free choice to repent of sin and do good works. The Valentinians also cannot say that the soul in question is under divine care from the moment of its creation, and later on is possessed by the demons, since this implies that at one time or other God is unable to protect the soul.

Having shown the error of Valentinus's teaching about demonic possession, Clement goes on to describe how the desire for pleasure fills the human soul with passions, just as moisture condenses above a marshland to cover the sky with clouds. Continued indulgence in fleshly pleasures also increases the power of the passions until the latter overwhelm the rational faculty of the soul and give it a bad disposition. Besieged by evil impulses, the soul can only become pure once the passions have been removed from it, much like pure gold is obtained when the slag is separated from the ore. Jesus himself illustrated the way in which the soul can purify itself by telling people that all those who ask for divine help will receive it. Even Barnabas, the co-worker of Paul, says that sinful people imitate the passionate behavior of the demons, not that spirits inhabit the soul. Indeed, Barnabas only speaks about

God living in the souls of baptized persons to indicate metaphorically how Christians keep the divine commandments and the promise of salvation in their hearts.[15]

The Polemic against the Valentinians

Although Valentinus is not mentioned anywhere else in the extant works of Clement, the teachings of his disciples are the subject of discussion in a brief section of book two of the *Stromateis*. There Clement attacks the Valentinians for making a distinction between Christians who are spiritual and those who are psychic in nature at the same time that he criticizes the Basilideans for their concept of faith as an innate quality of the elect. Clement opposes the Valentinian doctrine of two natures because it contradicts the fact that people can freely choose to believe in Christ or not and thus eliminates the need for the salvivic work of God, Jesus, and the church. What Clement finds most reprehensible about the Valentinian doctrine is that it makes God responsible for the nature, actions, and destiny of certain human beings.[16]

The criticism of Clement is also directed against the Valentinians at the beginning of the *Excerpta* when he borrows some of their language in order to refute their teachings about the nature of the church. After citing one of the Valentinian accounts of the spiritual seed or elect race put on by the Savior, Clement relates how he and his fellow Christians think that "the elect" (τὸ ἐκλεκτὸν) "seed" (σπέρμα) is a "spark" (σπινθῆρα) which is given life by the Logos. Clement draws upon material from several scriptural passages to add that the elect seed is also a "pupil of his eye", a "mustard seed", and the "leaven" which unites in faith the races that appear to be divided. Without admitting it, Clement has appropriated the words "the elect" (τὸ ἐκλεκτὸν), "seed" (σπέρμα), and "spark" (σπινθῆρα) from the Valentinians. Clement, however, reinterprets the meaning of these words to show how the Valentinians are mistaken in their assumption that they alone are "the elect" race or "seed" and that the "spark" is the spiritual element in their souls. Contrary to his opponents, Clement insists that the terms "the elect," "seed," and "spark" refer to every Christian who is given life by the Logos, and therefore, to the one church that unites the whole human race in faith.[17]

Clement continues his polemic against the Valentinians in a subsequent part of the *Excerpta* with a brief condemnation of their doctrine of the Paraclete. Following his discussion of their opinions on this subject, Clement explains how the Valentinians are unaware of the fact that the Paraclete and the Holy Spirit are one and the same, and that this spiritual entity has worked throughout history, inspiring not only the teachings of the Jewish law but those of the church. For Clement, unlike the followers of Valentinus, the teachings of the old and new testaments are in complete agreement because they were given by one Holy Spirit or Paraclete.[18]

Discussing aspects of the liturgy of the church in another one of his writings, Clement reinterprets some more language from the Valentinians in the *Excerpta* as a subtle way of contradicting their opinions on the twofold nature of baptism. In a brief passage of the *Eclogae Propheticae*, Clement says:

> ...since baptism takes place through water and Spirit, as a "protection against" (ἀλεξητήριον) the "twofold fire" (πυρὸς δισσοῦ)—both that which "takes hold of" (ἀπτομένου) invisible things, and that which takes hold of visible things—it is also necessary that there be "partly an intelligible" (τὸ μέν νοητόν) and "partly a sensible" (τὸ δὲ αἰσθητὸν) element of the water, as a protection against the twofold fire. And the earthly water cleanses the body; but the heavenly water is an allegorical expression of the Holy Spirit because it is intelligible and invisible—a purifier of invisible things....

Elsewhere, in the same text, Clement explains how baptism purifies the body and the soul and signifies the sanctification of our invisible element as well as the purification of the "unclean spirits" (πνεύματα ἀκάθαρτα) that are mixed up in our soul....[19]

From the preceding remarks, we can see how Clement has borrowed much of the Valentinian interpretation of the twofold nature of baptism given in the *Excerpta*. This is corroborated by the fact that Clement uses many of the same words as the Valentinians to describe baptism, including: "partly a sensible" (τὸ δὲ αἰσθητὸν), "partly an intelligible" (τὸ μέν νοητόν), "protection against" (ἀλεξητήριον), "twofold fire" (πυρὸς δισσοῦ), "takes hold of" (ἀπτομένου), and "unclean spirits" (πνεύματα ἀκάθαρτα). Nevertheless, Clement carefully changes the interpretation of the Valentinians to correct their idea that the baptismal water only serves as a protection against the sensible fire by driving the evil spirits from a person's soul. Against this notion, Clement asserts that the water of baptism puts out both the sensible and the intelligible fire—the first by washing the effects of sin from a person's body, and the second by eliminating the passions from their soul.

The problem of the relationship between spiritual entities and the human soul also occupies Clement in a passage of the *Excerpta* where he counters the Valentinians' claim about members of the spiritual race being identical in essence with the Holy Spirit. Clement follows up his quotation of the Valentinian statement on the identity of Jesus, Sophia, and the church by taking some material from Stoic philosophy and the scripture to argue:

...the human mixture in marriage produces the birth of one child from two seeds which have been mixed; and the body which is returned to the earth is mixed with the earth, as water with wine; but the better and superior bodies are capable of an easy mixture; wind, for example, is mixed with wind.

But it seems to me that this happens by juxtaposition, not by mixture. Therefore, when the divine power penetrates the soul, does it not sanctify the soul for the final advancement? For "God is Spirit"; he "breathes where he wishes". So the power does not penetrate by substance, but by power and strength; and the Spirit coexists with the spirit, as the spirit with the soul.[20]

By appealing to some categories from Stoic philosophy in the passage above Clement attempts to explain why the mixture of the human soul and the Holy Spirit as envisioned by the Valentinians is utterly impossible. Clement admits that such a mixture actually occurs when the sexual elements of a man and woman mingle together to produce a child, or when a dead body decays and dissolves into the surrounding earth. This kind of mixture also takes place when water is added to wine or a person's breath is blown into the wind. But when the Holy Spirit penetrates the soul of a person during baptism, it enters in the form of a spiritual power and not as a substance. Accordingly, the Holy Spirit coexists with the soul of the baptized person, just as the human soul and spirit live beside one another. In doing so the Holy Spirit neither becomes identified with nor makes any changes in the nature of a person's soul when they are baptized into the church.

The effects of baptism are the principal subject of yet another polemic ranged by Clement against the Valentinians in the first book of the *Paedagogus*. There Clement draws upon ideas found in various passages of the New Testament to contend:

and it is possible for us to strip from our abundance and to set to work against those who are fond of finding fault; for we are not called "children" and "infants" with regard to the childish and contemptible nature of our instruction, as those who are puffed up in knowledge slanderously claim. At any rate, when we were regenerated, we immediately received the perfection for which we strove. For we were enlightened and that is to know God. Therefore, he who knows perfection is not imperfect.[21]

After discussing the manner in which Jesus was made perfect through baptism, Clement extends the aforegoing criticism of the Valentinians by asserting:

...when we are baptized, we are enlightened; when we are enlightened, we are adopted as sons; when we are adopted as sons, we are perfected; when we are perfected, we are made immortal; it is written: "I have said: 'You are gods and all sons of the Most High.'" And this work is called in many ways a "gift," "enlightenment," "perfection," and "washing". It is a "washing" by which we cleanse ourselves of our sins, a "gift" by which the penalties caused by our sins are forgiven, and an "enlightenment" by which that holy light of salvation is beheld, that is, by which we clearly see the divine. And we call "perfect" that which is without want. For what can still be lacking for the one who knows God? It also is really absurd to say that what is not complete should be called a gift of God. But since God is perfect, he freely gives perfect things. And because all things were made by his command, so the perfecting of his grace follows his mere wish to give it freely. Thus the future of time is preceded by the power of his will.[22]

The purpose of Clement's argument in this passage of the *Paedagogus* is to show how the Valentinians are in error for thinking that they alone have attained spiritual perfection because of the knowledge imparted to them after baptism. Contradicting the criticism of his opponents, Clement argues that the scripture does not regard him and his fellow Christians as "children" and "infants" on account of the simplicity of their doctrine. This is demonstrated by the fact that when a person is spiritually reborn through baptism, they not only obtain perfect knowledge of God, but are adopted as sons of the divine, made complete with respect to salvation, and given the gift of immortality. Baptism also is called a "washing," a "gift," "enlightenment," and "perfection," since it eliminates the stains of sin from our bodies, releases us from punishment for our wrongdoing, allows us to see God, and saves us completely. Furthermore, baptism is the only means by which a person can receive the complete gift of salvation through the grace of God. This gift of salvation is complete because it is given by a perfect God, and it ensures the person who is baptized that they will be resurrected from the dead in the future.

Clement adds to his attack on the Valentinians in a subsequent section of the *Paedagogus* when he condemns his opponents' idea that a baptized person has not yet received the perfect gift of salvation. Quoting some material from the writings of Philo of Alexandria, Clement declares:

and I fully agree, except that he is in the light and the darkness does not overtake him. And there is nothing between the light and the darkness. The goal is laid up in the resurrection of those who believe; it is not the reception of some other thing, but rather obtaining the promise which was granted previously. So we say that "both cannot exist" together "at the same time"—"both arrival at the goal and" anticipation "of the arrival"; for eternity and time are not the same thing, nor are the starting point and the end; but both are about one thing, and one person is concerned with both. Accordingly, faith, so to speak, is the starting point which is born in time, and the end is gaining the promise which has been secured for eternity.[23]

Somewhat later, in the same part of the *Paedagogus* as above, Clement brings his argument against the Valentinians to a close by combining some ideas from pagan and Christian writings to state:

> and these chains are most quickly loosened by human faith and by divine grace, since sins are forgiven by one healing remedy—baptism in the Logos. Therefore, we wash away all of our sins, and immediately afterwards, we are no longer evil. This is the one grace of enlightenment: that our character is not the same as before washing. When that instruction formerly came to us, we, as ignorant pupils, also heard right away that knowledge rises up with enlightenment and illuminates the mind, though you might not be able to tell the time. For the catechetical instruction leads to faith; but faith is trained by the Holy Spirit together with baptism. Indeed, faith is the one universal salvation of humanity, and the equality and participation in the just and loving God are the same for all.... Consequently, there are not some who are Gnostics, and others who are psychics in the same Logos; but all those who have laid aside the fleshly desires are equal and spiritual before the Lord.[24]

These passages from the *Paedagogus* show Clement expressing agreement with the Valentinians that a person does not actually obtain eternal life at the time of their baptism. Nevertheless, Clement insists that a person does acquire knowledge of God when they are baptized and thus are never again in a state of complete or even partial ignorance about the divine. In addition, the goal of the Christian is to gain the eternal life which has been promised to those who have faith and are baptized, and not to receive esoteric instruction concerning God. As common sense dictates, a person cannot anticipate and arrive at the goal of eternal life at one and the same time, despite the fact that both anticipation and arrival are concerned with one thing—salvation—and one person—the believer. In light of this observation, it is clear that salvation starts with faith in this world and reaches its completion with eternal life in the world to come.

Clement ends his discussion by explaining how faith and grace liberate people from ignorance about God when their sins are forgiven through baptism.

The true power of baptism is demonstrated by the way it immediately enables a person to stop committing sin. In fact, those who are catechumens learn that their mind will be filled with knowledge of God during baptism even though no one knows exactly when this happens. Accordingly, the catechetical instruction before baptism leads a person to faith while the power of the Holy Spirit received during washing gives the faith of that person further training. Clement concludes that his opponents are wrong for saying that they alone know God and that other Christians like himself and his fellows are only simpletons concerned with faith. On the contrary, all human beings who are faithful and who have eliminated the passions from their souls will enjoy the promised gift of fellowship with God in the heavenly realm.

The polemic of Clement against the Valentinians takes a slightly different tack in the fourth book of the *Stromateis* as he criticizes the teachings of Heracleon on the subject of martyrdom. Just below his citation of the opinions of Heracleon, Clement collates material from various parts of the New Testament to say:

and with respect to other things he seems to agree with us in this section; but he has not considered the fact that if some have not confessed Christ in their conduct and life before men, they are shown by their disposition to have believed by confessing him with their voice in the courts and not denying him when tortured to death. And since this disposition is confessed and not even changed by death, it produces at once a cutting off of all the passions which were engendered by bodily desire. For there is, at the end of life, so to speak, almost a complete repentance in conduct and a true confession to Christ when the voice shall bear witness. And if "the Spirit of the Father" testifies in us, how can we still be hypocrites—we who are accused by him of testifying with the voice alone? If it is expedient, it shall be given to some to make a defense, so that both by their testimony and confession all might be helped: those in the church being made strong, those of the pagans who inquire into salvation being astonished and led to the faith, and the rest being seized by terror. So confession is completely necessary, for it is in our power; but making a defense is not absolutely required since it does not depend on us. "He who endures to the end shall be saved"; for who among those who think rightly would not choose to reign or even serve in the presence of God? Therefore, according to the apostle, some "confess that they know God, but deny him by their works, being abominable, disobedient, and unfit for any good deed." The latter are those who will have accomplished a single good work at the end, even if they only confess with their mouth. So it seems that their martyrdom is a purgation of sins with glory.[25]

Clement acknowledges in these remarks how he and his fellow Christians agree with Heracleon on some points concerning martyrdom, referring no doubt to their mutual distinction between two ways of confessing Christ and their emphasis upon the primary value of ethical conduct. Regardless of these points of agreement, Clement accuses Heracleon of not admitting that even if someone has denied Christ before men by acting in an unethical manner, they will be saved if they make a verbal confession of the Lord before a court of law and maintain that confession until death. The salvation of such a person is guaranteed because their verbal confession shows that they have eliminated the passions from their soul, repented of their sins, and manifested genuine faith in Christ. Furthermore, in contrast to the claims of Heracleon, a person who confesses Christ with their mouth before the courts cannot be a hypocrite, for their testimony is inspired by the Holy Spirit dwelling within them.

Describing his own role as a teacher in the church, Clement explains how God allows some people to defend the faith in court so their testimony might encourage other Christians to remain steadfast, bring some of the pagan spectators to salvation, and fill the judges with fear of being punished for persecuting those who are innocent. For this reason, all Christians must confess their faith in Christ if they are brought into court because it is within their power to do so. Only some, however, are required to defend the faith since that depends upon the will of God. Truly, the person who is wise will choose to endure persecution until death and enter into the presence of God even if that means that they will be among the least of those in heaven. In any case, those who uphold their confession of Christ unto death accomplish a good deed at the end of their lives and purge themselves of guilt for their former sins.

Clement rounds out his polemic against the Valentinians in the *Excerpta* by countering their eschatological doctrine with his own opinions on the nature and destiny of those who are saved. Just below the Valentinian description of the spiritual seeds ascending into the Pleroma, Clement employs the allegorical method of interpretation to claim:

when the high priest entered within the second veil, he laid the gold plate beside the altar of incense; and having the name engraved on his heart, he entered in silence.

Thus the high priest showed the laying aside of the body, which, like the gold plate, has become pure and light through the purification of the soul. On it was engraved the brightness of the piety by which he was known to the principalities and powers as one who wears the name.

He lays aside this body—the gold plate that has become without weight—within the second veil, within the intelligible world, which is the second complete veil of the universe. He lays it beside the altar of incense, with the angels who are ministers of the prayers which are lifted up.[26]

And the uncovered soul, which is in the power of the mind, and which has become like a body of the power, passes over into spiritual things. The soul now has become truly rational and high-priestly because it is directly animated, so to speak, by the Logos, just as the archangels have become high priests of the angels, and again, the first-created, high priests of the archangels.

And where is there still a perfection through the scripture and instruction for that soul which has become pure, since it is deemed worthy of seeing God "face to face"? Therefore, having passed beyond the angelic teaching and the name that is taught in the scripture, it comes to the knowledge and grasp of things. It is no longer a bride, but has already become a logos and rests with the bridegroom among the first-called and the first-created—those who have become friends because of love, sons because of the teaching and their obedience, and brothers because of the community of their origin.

So it belonged to the dispensation to wear the gold plate and learn with respect to knowledge; but it belongs to the power to make man become the bearer of God, being moved directly by the Lord and becoming like his body.[27]

The portrait of the ascent of the soul in the passage above is given by Clement as a corrective to the Valentinian teaching about the spiritual seeds entering the Pleroma. Clement begins by explaining that on the Day of Atonement, the Jewish high priest laid his gold breastplate beside the altar of incense and passed behind the second veil in the temple to enter the Holy of Holies with the name of God inscribed on his heart. By doing so the high priest gave a symbolic representation of the way in which the soul of a saved person places its physical body beside the angels who receive prayers and enters into the heavenly realm with the name of Christ upon it. As the high priest was known by the spiritual powers because of the purity of his body, so the soul of a saved person is recognized by the ministering angels on account of the purity of its body. In fact, the soul is the power of the mind of the saved person, and it becomes a spiritual body akin to that of the Logos-Christ once it passes into the intelligible world or heaven.

Since the soul is empowered by the Logos when it enters the heavenly realm, it becomes completely rational, and, like the first-created angels and archangels, acts as a high priest for the spiritual beings that exist below it. In this state the soul transcends the ethical perfection that it attained on earth by obeying the divine commandments in the scripture, and it is deemed worthy of contemplating the Only-begotten Son or face of God. Consequently, the soul is said to have gone beyond the teachings in the scripture and to have come to knowledge of the Father. The soul also is no longer a bride of Christ, but has become a logos and rests with the first-created angels and the other souls which have already been called to heaven. Thenceforth, the saved souls and the first-created angels reside together as friends, sons, and brothers due to their mutual love, obedience to the divine commandments, and creation by God. Clement concludes that the soul is placed in a physical body to acquire some knowledge of God, but it becomes a spiritual body when it is given power in heaven by the Logos. Thus Clement, unlike his Valentinian opponents, argues that the soul of every human being is capable of ascending into the heavenly realm, resting with the bridegroom Christ, and contemplating the Father forever, once it has been saved by faith, baptism, and good works. Unlike the Valentinians, Clement further believes that even though the saved soul will be elevated to the rank of the first-created angels, it will only contemplate the Father through the mediation of the Son.

Notes

[1] *Strom.* 7.106.4-7.3 (3.75.13–76.4); 108.1-2 (3.76.20–4). On the idea of Basilides establishing his Christian community after the founding of the original church see Hegesippus cited in Eus. *H.E.* 4.22.4–6; Iren. *Adv. Haer.* 3.2.1; 4.3.

[2] *Strom.* 5.3.2–3 (2.327.22f.; 24f.). On faith as voluntary assent see also *Strom.* 2.8.4 (2.117.8f.); 2.9.1–2 (2.117.12–5); 5.86.1 (2.383.1).

[3] *Strom.* 5.3.3–4.1 (2.327.25–28.8). On Abraham under the oak in Mamre see Gen. 18.1; on the land given "to you" "and to your seed" see Gen. 17.8; on "it was reckoned to him" see Gen. 15.6; Rom. 4.3. See also Le Boulluec, *Les Stromates: Stromate* 5, p. 29 on belief as proof of election.

[4] *Strom.* 2.165.4 (2.321.30-3). On those who are strangers on the earth see Heb. 11.13.

[5] *Strom.* 4.83.2–85.2 (2.285.6–29); cf. *Strom.* 4.73.5–74.1 (2.281.14–8).

[6] *Strom.* 4.85.3–88.5 (2.285.31–87.8); on mortifying the desires see Col. 3.5; cf. *Strom.* 7.81.2 (3.58.2f.); on "I shall tear down the wall" see Is. 5.5; cf. 1 Thess. 4.3–8; Iren. *Adv. Haer.* 1.24.6.

[7] *Strom.* 4.153.4–54.4 (2.316.16–30). On "you thought, lawless one" see Ps. 49.21; on the idea that what is done cannot be undone see Plato *Leg.* 11.934ab; *Prot.* 324b; cf. *Strom.* 4.153.2–4 (2.316.11–4); on punishment helping a person to sin no longer or, by way of example, helping someone else not to sin see Plato *Leg.* 11.934ab; *Prot.* 324b; cf. *Strom.* 1.168.3 (2.104.29); on the things which were practiced first being forgiven through baptism see Acts 2.38; 3.19; 22.16; cf. Eph. 5.26f.; Tit. 3.3ff..

[8] *Strom.* 2.11.1-2 (2.118.21-19.3). On voluntary and involuntary acts see Chrysipp. *Fr. Phys.* 988 Arnim.

[9] *Strom.* 2.27.1–2 (2.127.18f.).

[10] *Strom.* 3.3.3–4.3 (2.196.17-97.15). On "false apostles" and "whose end shall be like their works" see 2 Cor. 11.13, 15; cf. *Strom.* 3.59.1–2 (2.223.5–8); on desiring only what is necessary see Epicurus *Fr.* 456 Usener; cf. Plato *Leg.* 848a; Arist. *Eth. Nich.* 7.4; on continence as a divine grace or gift see *1 Clem.* 38.2; cf. Ign. *Polyc.* 5.2 cited in Chadwick, *Alexandrian Christianity*, p. 42 n.9; on sexual abstinence see 1 Cor. 7.1, 8, 37f.; cf. Athenag. *Leg.* 33; on one marriage see 1 Cor. 7.2, 9f., 39; on "bear the burdens" see Gal. 6.2; on "who thinks that he stands" see 1 Cor. 10.12; on a second marriage see 1 Cor. 7.9, 36, 38; cf. *Strom.* 3.82.4–5 (2.233.25–9).

[11] *Ecl.* 17.1 (3.141.19f.).

[12] *Strom.* 7.106.4-107.1 (3.75.13ff., 17); 107.2-3 (3.76.1-4); 108.1 (3.76.20f.). See *Strom.* 6.53.1 (2.458.16ff.) where Clement explains how Valentinus has made the truth common to all people by saying that the teachings of the church appear in Jewish or other non-Christian books. Although Clement would agree with Valentinus that the teachings of the church are foreshadowed in some ancient Jewish and Greek books, he would not say, as does the former, that such teachings are the exclusive possession of the spiritual race.

[13] *Strom.* 5.3.3–4.1 (2.327.25-28.8); cf. Gen. 18.1; 17.8; 15.6; Rom. 4.3. On belief as proof of election see Le Boulluec, *Les Stromates: Stromate* 5, p. 29.

[14] *Strom.* 2.115.1-3 (2.175.15-23).

[15] *Strom.* 2.115.3-17.5 (2.175.23-76.22). On Jesus' statement see Matt. 7.7; Luke 11.9. Note that the form of "ask" (αἰτεῖσθε), which is used by Clement here, appears in Mark 11.24, but not in the passages of Matthew and Luke cited above. On the comments supposedly made by Barnabas see *Barn.* 16.7-8.

[16] *Strom.* 2.11.1-2 (2.118.21–119.3). On voluntary and involuntary acts see Chrysipp. *Fr. Phys.* 988 Arnim. It is of interest to note that Clement's doctrine of free will here stands in opposition to the doctrine of predestination developed by the onetime Manichaean, Augustine. On the relationship between Augustine's ideas and those of the Gnostics in general see Rudolph, *Gnosis,* 370f..

[17] *Exc.* 1.3. On the Valentinian language in this passage see "the elect," "seed," and "spark" in *Exc.* 1.2; 3.1-2; on the "pupil of his eye" see Deut. 32.10; on the "mustard seed" see Matt. 13.31; on the "leaven" see Matt. 13.33; Luke 13.21.

[18] *Exc.* 24.2; cf. *Exc.* 19.2; *Ecl.* 23.1-3 (3.143.4-11).

[19] *Ecl.* 8.1-2 (3.138.33–39.6); *Ecl.* 7.2-3 (3.138.29ff.). On the Valentinian language in this passage see "partly a sensible," "partly an intelligible," "protection against," "twofold fire," "takes hold of," and "unclean spirits" in the soul in *Exc.* 81.1-3; 77.3; 83-4. On baptism through water and the Spirit see John 3.5; 1.33; cf. Gen. 1.2; on the purification or sanctification of the soul see 1 Pet. 1.22; on the purification or sanctification through baptism see Eph. 5.26; cf. Heb. 10.22; 1 Cor. 6.11.

[20] *Exc.* 17.2-4. On "God is Spirit" and "breathes where he wishes" see John 4.24; 3.8; on the various types of mixture identified by Stoic philosophers see the discussion in Sagnard, *Extr. de Théod.,* p. 216.

[21] *Paed.* 1.25.1 (1.104.25–105.3); cf. *Paed.* 1.27.3 (1.106.15ff.); *Paed.* 1.39.1 (1.113.9ff.). On those who are "infants" see 1 Cor. 3.1; cf. Heb. 5.13; on knowledge that puffs up see 1 Cor. 8.1; on regeneration see 1 Pet. 1.3, 23; Titus 3.5; on perfection see Heb. 2.10; 5.9; 7.11, 28; cf. James 1.17; on those who are enlightened see Heb. 6.4; 10.32. Although Clement does not give a specific name for his opponents in this section of the *Paedagogus,* his references to their distinction between "Gnostics" and "psychics" in the church and emphasis on knowledge given after baptism indicates that they were Valentinians; cf. *Paed.* 1.31.2 (1.108.23-6); *Strom.* 2.10.2-3 (2.118.13-7); *Exc.* 56.2-3; 58.1; 78.2.

[22] *Paed.* 1.26.1-3 (1.105.20–106.1). On being adopted as sons see Gal. 4.5-7; on the quote see Ps. 81.6; cf. John 10.34; on the "gift" of God as eternal life see Rom. 5.15; 6.23; cf. James 1.17; on "enlightenment" and "perfection" see Heb. 2.10; 5.9; 7.11, 28; 6.4; 10.32; on the "washing" see Titus 3.5; cf. Eph. 5.26; on God creating by his command see Ps. 32.9; 148.5.

[23] *Paed.* 1.28.3-5 (1.106.30–107.8). On darkness not overtaking him see John 1.5; on the quote see Philo *De Agric.* 161.

[24] *Paed.* 1.29.5-30.2; 31.2 (1.107.33–108.12, 23–6). On the healing remedy see Paean in *Il.* 5.401f. cited in Roberts and Donaldson, edd., *The Ante-Nicene Fathers,* vol. 2, p. 216; on laying aside the fleshly desires see 1 Pet. 2.1, 11; on those who are Gnostics see also *Paed.* 1.52.2 (1.121.8f.).

[25] *Strom.* 4.73.1–74.4 (2.281.3-26). On "the Spirit of the Father" see Matt. 10.20; on some being given what to say in defense see Mark 13.11; Matt. 10.19f.; Luke 12.11f.; on "he who endures" see Matt. 10.22; 24.13; Mark 13.13; on those who

"confess that they know God" see Tit. 1.16.

[26] *Exc.* 27.1-2; cf. *Strom.* 5.33.1-2 (2.347.11–4). On the allegorical interpretation of the high priest entering the Holy of Holies see Philo *De Vit. Mos.* 2.101; 115; 132; on the Holy of Holies behind the second veil see Heb. 9.3; Lev. 16.2; Ex. 26.33f.; on the high priest wearing a gold plate see Lev. 8.9; Ex. 28.36f.; on the altar of incense see Ex. 30.1; on the ascent of the purified soul into heaven see Plato *Rep.* 10.614b–15b; on the second veil as the entrance to the intelligible world see Philo *De Vit. Mos.* 2.82; on the connection between the altar of incense and the angels ministering to prayer see Philo *De Vit. Mos.* 102.3. On Clement's dependence upon Philo for his description of the high priest here and in *Strom.* 5.32.1–40.4 (2.346.27–54.4) see the references noted in Stählin, *Clemens Alexandrinus,* vol. 2, pp. 347–53; Mondésert, *Clement d'Alexandrie,* pp. 172–81; Sagnard, *Extr. de Théod.,* pp. 220–3.

[27] *Exc.* 27.3-6; cf. *Strom.* 2.134.2 (2.187.9f.); 7.5.6 (3.6.6f.); 7.21.2–3 (3.15.16f.). On the power of God as the Logos see 1 Cor. 1.24; on the soul becoming high-priestly see the Logos as the high priest in Philo *De Vit. Mos.* 2.133f.; *De Spec. Leg.* 5.20; 6.96; 11.6; on "face to face" see 1 Cor. 13.12; cf. Matt. 5.8; *Exc.* 11.2; 15.2; 23.4–5; on the saved soul or person as a bride see John 3.29; cf. Rev. 22.17; on the saved soul or person as a logos see *Exc.* 25.1; 64; on the saved soul or person resting see Heb. 4.1ff., 8–12; cf. Matt. 11.28f.; Philo *De Fuga* 174; on Jesus as the bridegroom see John 3.29; on those who are saved being friends because of love see John 15.12–5; on those who are saved being sons of God see Ps. 81.6; cf. John 10.34; *Paed.* 1.26.2 (1.105.22); on those who are saved being children of God because of their obedience to divine teaching see Heb. 2.1-4, 10-4; cf. John 1.12f.; on those who are saved being brothers because they have the same origin see Heb. 2.11f.. I do not accept the supposition that *Exc.* 27 is from a "gnostic author," as stated by S. Lilla in his otherwise excellent book, *Clement of Alexandria,* pp. 176–9. In contrast to the arguments adduced by Lilla in favor of the Gnostic authorship of *Exc.* 27: 1) the notion of the soul's heavenly journey does appear in non-Gnostic texts of the period; 2) the use of passwords is not discussed in *Exc.* 27; 3) the powers and principalities are not said to rule over the heavens in *Exc.* 27; 4) the body, not the soul, is laid aside in *Exc.* 27; 5) the soul rather than a spiritual element enters heaven and becomes a bride in *Exc.* 27; 6) the idea of the soul as a bride can also be inferred from the Gospel of John or Revelation; 7) heaven is not called a "bridal chamber" in *Exc.* 27; 8) the idea of a brotherhood based on a common origin also appears in the Epistle to the Hebrews; and 9) the saved are not "friends" and "sons" because of knowledge in *Exc.* 27, but because of love, teaching, and obedience, as described, for instance, in the Epistle to the Hebrews.

Conclusion

THE first two chapters of our study indicate that Clement knew a great deal about the teachings of Basilides, Valentinus, and their respective followers, as evidenced by the number of citations from their writings and summaries of their doctrines which he makes in the *Paedagogus*, *Stromateis*, and *Excerpta ex Theodoto*. Sometimes Clement gives quotations from specific books of Basilides and Isidore or the letters and homilies of Valentinus. In other places, without naming a particular written source, Clement quotes or describes what various Basilideans and Valentinians have said. Although it is impossible to know exactly where Clement got his information in these passages, he probably took it from the writings of the Basilideans and Valentinians, from anthologies of "heretical" teachings known to have circulated among certain churches in the second century, or from the works of another heresiologist like Irenaeus. Regardless of the sources used by Clement, there is no reason to doubt the authenticity of the material which he attributes to his opponents. Indeed, Clement is considered to be one of our most trustworthy sources on the teachings of the Basilideans and Valentinians because he gives so many quotations from their writings and refrains from distorting their teachings in order to support his polemic against them.

In our discussion we have learned how Clement cites the teachings of the Basilideans and Valentinians for the sole purpose of refuting them. When Clement responds directly to the opinions of his opponents in the *Paedagogus*, *Stromateis*, and *Excerpta*, his remarks are invariably critical. Even in the *Excerpta* where Clement does not directly address the Valentinians, he is clearly setting forth his own ideas in opposition to theirs. In fact, we have demonstrated how in the *Stromateis*, *Excerpta*, *Eclogae*, and *Hypotyposes*, Clement borrows some of the language and ideas of the Valentinians so he can reinterpret such material against them. At no point in his extant writings does Clement ever express any unqualified approval of the teachings of Basilides, Valentinus, or their disciples. Instead, he always refers to these people as "heretics" or teachers of false doctrine.

As we have shown, Clement attacks the Basilideans and Valentinians for their teachings on the nature of God, the Savior, creation, and the church. In contrast to the dualism and determinism of his opponents Clement insists on the unity of God, the Savior, the human race, and the church as well as the freedom of human beings to choose to believe and obey the divine commandments. Clement also refutes the docetism of the Valentinian Christology by emphasizing the physical reality of the body of Jesus Christ while rejecting the Basilidean doctrine of reincarnation by arguing that the human soul only enters the body and the world one time. With respect to other questions, Clement upholds the teachings of Jesus and Paul on marriage to castigate the libertinism of certain Basilideans and consistently affirms the essential goodness of God, the creation, and the human body and soul against the pessimism of his opponents. Lastly, Clement rejects the elitism of both the Basilideans and Valentinians by asserting that all human beings can be saved through faith, baptism, and good works, and enjoy the rewards of salvation in the same heavenly realm with the Father and the Son.

On the whole, Clement criticizes his opponents by explaining how their ideas are illogical, contradict the scripture, or have negative implications for other aspects of Christian belief and practice. Clement usually maintains his composure while addressing his opponents, though occasionally his language becomes somewhat emotional, particularly when he attacks the doctrine of martyrdom held by Basilides or the sexual and marital practices of the libertines. Only in a couple of places does Clement actually level unfair accusations against his opponents, namely, when he charges Basilides with deifying the Devil and the Basilideans with calling the Ruler, "the greatest" god. Nevertheless, even in these instances, Clement's exaggerated rhetoric and incorrect information are offset by the overall clarity and validity of his main arguments.

Despite our lack of demographic information on religious groups in the ancient world, the Basilidean and Valentinian congregations were probably some of the largest and most influential of the Christian communities in Alexandria at the end of the second century. To be sure, Clement conducted his polemic against the disciples of Basilides and Valentinus not only to persuade them to abandon their false beliefs and practices, but to prevent them from converting members of his own church over to their communities. Whether Clement succeeded in convincing many of his opponents to join him and his fellow Christians is unknown. What is clear, however, is that Clement maintained the catechetical school founded by Pantaenus and provided that institution with an invaluable outline of "orthodox" Christian philosophy in contrast to the "heretical" systems of thought espoused by his opponents. The success of Clement's work as a teacher and writer is illustrated by the fact that the catechetical school continued to operate long after his departure from Alexandria and played a significant role in establishing the primacy of catholic Christianity in Egypt.

There is no doubt that Clement's voluminous writings constitute his greatest contribution to the church. In these writings Clement creates a comprehensive Christian philosophy which surpasses that of the Basilideans and Valentinians both in its intellectual acumen and its doctrinal orthodoxy. Throughout his literary works Clement also demonstrates the importance of education and learning for the Christian church and proves that the quest for knowledge about the nature of God, the world, and humankind does not necessitate falling into heretical error. Generally speaking, the philosophy of Clement is more appealing than that of his opponents because it emphasizes the goodness of the creation and the reality of free will, and thereby validates collective and individual human experience. The best part of Clement's philosophy is his belief in the inherent worth of all human beings and the possibility of universal salvation, ideas that certainly made his brand of Christianity most attractive to potential converts.

Though Clement does not explicitly state this in his extant writings, he clearly was acquainted with bishop Demetrius and supported the ecclesiastical program of the latter through his teaching and writing at the catechetical school. Clement exhibits his allegiance to the catholic orthodoxy of Demetrius, and perhaps even the influence of Irenaeus's *Adversus Haereses*, when he champions ideas about the unity of the original church and its apostolic doctrine against the ecclesiology of the Basilideans and Valentinians. By identifying his own Christian community with the one true church and claiming to have exclusive possession of the apostolic doctrine Clement certainly helped to consolidate power in the hands of Demetrius and the nascent catholic church of Alexandria.

From a broader perspective, we can see how some of the ideas which Clement borrowed from the Valentinians were to play an important role in the subsequent development of the doctrine and organization of the church. On the one hand, the notion of the Savior's special body foreshadows the emphasis on the divinity of Jesus among the Monophysites and the resulting Christological controversies of the sixth century. Similarly, the idea of the elect as a superior rank within the church finds its fullest expression in the monastic movement where a select few were presumed to have attained the status of a spiritual elite both on earth and in heaven. Finally, the distinction between the elect and the called members of the church looks forward to the eventual separation of the clergy from the laity in the eastern and western churches. An investigation of the possible connections between these ideas taken by Clement from the Valentinians and those of Christians in the following centuries is a subject for another study. It is of some interest to note, however, that certain Valentinian doctrines appropriated by Clement anticipated some things to come in the history of the church.

Selected Bibliography

Texts and Translations

Butterworth, G.W. ed. *Clement of Alexandria*. Loeb Classical Library. Cambridge, Mass.: Harvard University Press, 1919.

Casey, R.P. ed. *The Excerpta ex Theodoto of Clement of Alexandria*. London: Christophers, 1934.

Foerster, W. ed. *Gnosis: A Selection of Gnostic Texts*, 2 vols. Eng. trans. ed. R.McL. Wilson. Oxford: Oxford University Press, 1972, 1974.

Grant, R.M. *Second Century Christianity: A Collection of Fragments*. London: S.P.C.K., 1957.

Layton, B. ed. *The Gnostic Scriptures*. Garden City: Doubleday and Company, Inc., 1987.

Marrou, H.I. and Harl, M. edd. *Le Pédagogue I*. Sources Chrétiennes 70. Paris: Éditions du Cerf, 1960.

Mondésert, C. and Camelot, P. edd. *Les Stromates: Stromate II*. Sources Chrétiennes 38. Paris: Éditions du Cerf, 1954.

—— and Caster, P. edd. *Les Stromates: Stromate I*. Sources Chrétiennes 30. Paris: Éditions du Cerf, 1951.

—— and Marrou, H.I. edd. *Le Pédagogue II*. Sources Chrétiennes 108. Paris: Éditions du Cerf, 1965.

——, Matray, C. and Marrou, H.I. edd. *Le Pédagogue III*. Sources Chrétiennes 158. Paris: Éditions du Cerf, 1970.

—— and Plassart, A. edd. *Le Protreptique*. Sources Chrétiennes 2, 2nd ed. Paris: Éditions du Cerf, 1961.

Nestle, E. and Aland, K. edd. *Novum Testamentum Graece et Latine*. Stuttgart: Deutsche Bibelgesellschaft, 1979.

Oulton, J.E.L. and Chadwick, H. edd. *Alexandrian Christianity*. Philadelphia: The Westminster Press, 1954.

Rahlfs, A. ed. *Septuaginta*. Stuttgart: Deutsche Bibelgesellschaft, 1935, 1979.

Roberts, A. and Donaldson, J. edd. *The Ante-Nicene Fathers*, vol. 2. William Wilson trans. of Clement of Alexandria. Grand Rapids: Eerdmans, 1979.

Robinson, J.M. ed. *The Coptic Gnostic Library: Nag Hammadi Codices I-XIII*, 13 vols. The Institute for Antiquity and Christianity. Leiden: E. J. Brill, 1970– .

————. *The Nag Hammadi Library in English*. Leiden: E. J. Brill, 1977.

Sagnard, F. ed. *Les Extraits de Théodote*. Sources Chrétiennes 23. Paris: Éditions du Cerf, 1948.

Smith, M. *Clement of Alexandria and a Secret Gospel of Mark*. Cambridge, Mass.: Harvard University Press, 1973.

Stählin, Otto ed. *Clemens Alexandrinus*, 4 vols. Newly edited vols. 1 and 4 by Ursula Treu and vols. 2 and 3 by Ludwig Früchtel. Berlin: Akademie-Verlag, 1960–80.

————. trans. *Des Clemens von Alexandreia ausgewählte Schriften*, 5 vols. Bibliothek der Kirchenvater. München: Kösel-Verlag KG, 1934–8; Nendeln: Kraus Reprint, 1968.

Voulet, P. ed. *Les Stromates: Stromates V*. Sources Chrétiennes 278. Paris: Éditions du Cerf, 1981.

Wood, Simon P. trans. *Christ the Educator*. Washington, D.C.: The Catholic University of America Press, 1954.

Studies

Arndt, W.F., Gingrich, F.W., and Danker F.W. edd. *A Greek-English Lexicon of the New Testament and Other Early Christian Literature*, 2nd ed. A translation and adaptation of the fifth revised and augmented edition of W. Bauer's *Griechisch-Deutsches Wörterbuch zu den Schriften des*

Neuen Testaments und der übrigen urchristlichen Literatur. Chicago: Chicago University Press, 1979.

Bigg, C. *The Christian Platonists of Alexandria*, 2nd ed. Oxford: Oxford University Press, 1913; repr. 1968.

Buonaiuti, E. "Symbols and Rites in the Religious Life of Certain Monastic Orders," *The Mystic Vision: Papers from the Eranos Yearbooks*, ed. J. Campbell. Princeton: Princeton University Press, 1968, pp. 168–209.

Butterworth, G.W. "The Deification of Man in Clement of Alexandria," *Journal of Theological Studies* 17 (1916) 157–69.

Casey, R.P. "Clement of Alexandria and the Beginnings of Christian Platonism," *Harvard Theological Review* 18 (1925) 39–101.

——. "Two Notes on Valentinian Theology," *Harvard Theological Review* 25 (1930) 275–98.

Chadwick, H. *Early Christian Thought and the Classical Tradition: Studies in Justin, Clement, and Origen.* New York: Oxford University Press, 1966.

——. "Clement of Alexandria," *The Cambridge History of Later Greek and Early Medieval Philosophy*, ed. A.H. Armstrong. Cambridge: Cambridge University Press, 1967, pp. 168–81.

Clark, E.A. *Clement's Use of Aristotle.* New York: Edwin Mellen Press, 1977.

Cross, F.L. and Livingstone, E.A. edd. *The Oxford Dictionary of the Christian Church*, 2nd ed. Oxford: Oxford University Press, 1983.

Davison, J.E. "Structural Similarities and Dissimilarities in the Thought of Clement of Alexandria and the Valentinians," *The Second Century: A Journal of Early Christian Studies* Winter (1983) 201–17.

Dibelius, O. "Studien zur Geschichte der Valentinianer, I: Die Excerpta ex Theodoto und Irenäus," *Zeitschrift für die neutestamentliche Wissenschaft* 9 (1908) 230–47.

Dillon, J.M. *The Middle Platonists.* London: Duckworth, 1977.

Egan, J. "Logos and Emanation in the Writings of Clement of Alexandria," *Trinification of the World: A Festschrift in Honor of Frederick E. Crowe*, edd. T.A. Dunne and J.M. Laporte. Toronto: Regis College Press, 1978, pp. 176–209.

Festugière, A.J. "Notes sur les Extraits de Théodote de Clément d' Alexandrie et sur les Fragments de Valentin," *Vigiliae Christianae* 3 (1949) 193–207.

Foerster, W. *Von Valentin zu Herakleon: Untersuchungen über die Quellen und die Entwicklung der valentinianischen Gnosis.* Beihefte zur Zeitschrift für die neutestamentliche Wissenschaft und die Kunde der alteren Kirche 7. Giessen: Alfred Töpelmann, 1928.

———. "Das System des Basilides," *New Testament Studies* 9 (1963) 233–55.

Frend, W.H.C. *Martyrdom and Persecution in the Early Church.* New York: New York University Press, 1967.

———. *The Rise of Christianity.* Philadelphia: Fortress Press, 1984.

Grant, R.M. "Place de Basilide dans la théologie chrétienne ancienne," *Revue des études augustiniennes* 25 (1979) 201–16.

Jonas, H. *The Gnostic Religion*, 2nd ed. rev. Boston: Beacon Press, 1963.

Kirk, G.S., Raven, J.E., and Schofield, M. *The Presocratic Philosophers.* Cambridge: Cambridge University Press, 1983.

Koester, H. *Introduction to the New Testament: History, Culture, and Religion of the Hellenistic Age.* Philadelphia: Fortress Press, 1982.

Lampe, G.W.H. ed. *A Patristic Greek Lexicon.* Oxford: Oxford University Press, 1961.

Lattey, Cuthbert. "The Deification of Man in Clement of Alexandria: Some Further Notes," *Journal of Theological Studies* 17 (1916) 257–62.

Layton, B. ed. *The Rediscovery of Gnosticism: Proceedings of the Conference at Yale, March 1978*, 2 vols. Vol. I: The School of Valentinus. Vol. II: Sethian Gnosticism. Leiden: E. J. Brill, 1980, 1981.

Le Boulluec, A. *Les Stromates: Stromate V*. Sources Chrétiennes 279. Paris: Éditions du Cerf, 1981.

Liddell, H.G., Scott, R., and Jones H.S. edd. *A Greek-English Lexicon*, 9th ed. Oxford: Oxford University Press, repr. 1983.

Lilla, Salvatore R.C. *Clement of Alexandria: A Study in Christian Platonism and Gnosticism*. Oxford: Oxford University Press, 1971.

Méhat, A. *Etude sur Les 'Stromates' de Clément d' Alexandrie*. Patristica Sorbonensia 7. Paris: Éditions du Seuil, 1966.

Mondésert, C. *Clément d' Alexandrie: Introduction a l' étude de sa pensée religieuse a parti de l' ecriture*. Paris: Editions Montaigne, 1944.

Mortley, R. *Connaissance religieuse et hermeneutique chez Clément d' Alexandrie*. Leiden: E. J. Brill, 1973.

——— . "The Theme of Silence in Clement of Alexandria," *Journal of Theological Studies* XXIV (1973) 197–202.

——— . "The Mirror and 1 Cor. 13,12 in the Epistemology of Clement of Alexandria," *Vigiliae Christianae* 30 (1976) 109–120.

Nautin, Pierre. "Les fragments de Basilide sur la souffrance et leur interprétation par Clément d' Alexandrie et Origène," *Mélanges d' histoire des religions offerts à Henri-Charles Puech*. Paris: Presses universitaires de France, 1974, pp. 393–403.

——— . "La fin des *Stromates* et les *Hypotyposes* de Clément d' Alexandrie," *Vigiliae Christianae* 30 (1976) 268–302.

Osborn, E.F. *The Philosophy of Clement of Alexandria*. Cambridge: Cambridge University Press, 1957.

——— . "Clement of Alexandria: A Review of Research, 1958–1982," *The Second Century: A Journal of Early Christian Studies* Winter (1983) 219–44.

Outler, A.C. "The 'Platonism' of Clement of Alexandria," *The Journal of Religion* (1940) 217–40.

Pearson, B.A. *Gnosticism, Judaism, and Egyptian Christianity.* Studies in Antiquity and Christianity. Minneapolis: Fortress Press, 1990.

Puech, H.-C. "Gnosis and Time," *Man and Time: Papers from the Eranos Yearbooks*, ed. J. Campbell. Princeton: Princeton University Press, 1957, pp. 38–84.

Quispel, G. "The Original Doctrine of Valentine," *Vigiliae Christianae* 1 (1947) 43–73.

———. "Gnostic Man: The Doctrine of Basilides," *The Mystic Vision: Papers from the Eranos Yearbooks*, ed. J. Campbell. Princeton: Princeton University Press, 1968, pp. 210–46.

Rudolph, K. *Gnosis: The Nature and History of Gnosticism.* Trans. edited by R.McL. Wilson. San Francisco: Harper and Row, 1983.

Sagnard, F. *La Gnose valentinienne et le témoignage de Saint Irénée.* Études de philosophie médiévale, vol. 36. Paris: J. Vrin, 1947.

Solmsen, F. "Providence and the Souls: A Platonic Chapter in Clement of Alexandria," *Museum Helveticum*, vol. 26, Fasc. 4, October (1969) 229–51.

Stead, G.C. "The Valentinian Myth of Sophia," *Journal of Theological Studies* n.s. 20 (1969) 75–104.

Tollinton, R.B. *Clement of Alexandria: A Study in Christian Liberalism*, 2 vols. London: Williams and Norgate, 1914.

Völker, W. *Der wahre Gnostiker nach Clemens Alexandrinus.* Texte und Untersuchungen 57. Berlin, 1952.

Wagner, W. "A Father's Fate: Attitudes and Interpretations of Clement of Alexandria," *Journal of Religious History* 7 (1971) 209–31.

Wlosok, A. *Laktanz und die philosophische Gnosis: Untersuchungen zu Geschichte und Terminologie der gnostischen Erlosungsvorstellung.* Abhandlungen der Heidelberger Akademie der Wissenschaften, Philosophisch-historische Klasse 2. Heidelberg: Carl Winter Universitätsverlag, 1960.

Wolfson, H. A. *The Philosophy of the Church Fathers*, vol. 1, 3rd ed. rev. Cambridge, Mass.: Harvard University Press, 1956.

Wytzes, J. "Paideia and Pronoia in the Works of Clemens Alexandrinus," *Vigiliae Christianae* 9 (1955) 146–58.

———. "The Twofold Way. Platonic Influences in the Work of Clement of Alexandria," *Vigiliae Christianae* 11 (1957) 226–45; 14 (1960) 129–53.